Solicitors' Guide to Good Management

Practical management checklists for lawyers

Trevor Boutall and Bill Blackburn

The Law Society

First edition published 1996
This second edition published 2001
Reprinted 2002, 2003, 2004, 2005 and 2006

ISBN 1-85328-732-6

The authors are grateful for the help of Sue Eccleston, Sarah Foulkes, Karen Harley, Tracey Stanley, Maxine Warr and Jane Withey in the preparation of this edition.

Published by the Law Society
113 Chancery Lane, London WC2A 1PL

Text design by BarkerHilsdon
Printed and bound in Great Britain by MPG Books Ltd, Bodmin, Cornwall

Contents

Contents

Contents

Preface

This guide is for all solicitors whether or not they consider themselves to be involved in practice management. Office administration may be delegated to a specialist in some practices, but senior lawyers are necessarily involved in managing staff and in managing their case load. The most junior assistant has some case management responsibility and often manages some relations with clients. Whether they are in private practice or in a legal department, all solicitors must manage their time and their relations with colleagues.

The book is an adaptation of the *Good Manager's Guide*, second edition (Boutall 1997) which was published by the Management Charter Initiative (MCI) to provide a series of practical checklists for managers. The checklists of the *Good Manager's Guide* are based upon the national Management Standards which describe the standards of performance expected of all managers and supervisors. The national Management Standards apply to managers and supervisors, regardless of where they work. The context may be different, but the process of, say, budgeting, or hiring or dismissing people is similar in all sectors.

It was noted that the checklists contained in the *Good Manager's Guide* could, if suitably adapted, be used by any solicitor confronted by a management task. The adaptation has been carried out by Trevor Boutall, the author of the *Good Manager's Guide*, and Bill Blackburn, a solicitor with a background in commerce and private practice.

The Law Society has developed the Practice Management Standards. Practices and legal departments that have been independently assessed as having achieved these standards may be certified under the Law Society's Lexcel scheme. The Law Society has published a *Lexcel Office Procedures Manual* (Moore and Dodd 2001) to provide a template to enable any legal practice to implement systems and procedures that meet the Practice Management Standards. The checklists contained in the *Good Manager's Guide* have, therefore, been further expanded and adapted to ensure that they are fully compatible with the Practice Management Standards.

This guide is directed primarily to the needs of solicitors in private practice but lawyers in local government or commerce and industry will find it useful. It is also designed to help individual lawyers, particularly if they are not themselves closely involved in the management of a practice. Lawyers and others having, or assuming, responsibility for the management of a practice will certainly find the checklists helpful. They are, however, referred for further essential guidance to the *Lexcel Office Procedures Manual* and, if appropriate, *Setting Up and Managing a Small Practice* (Smith 1995).

Please see the further reading chapter at the end of this book for full details of the books mentioned throughout this guide and how to obtain them.

The next steps

To obtain a copy of the national Management Standards, advice and guidance on National Vocational Qualifications (NVQs), or advice and guidance concerning management training generally, contact:

> Management Standards Unit
> 3rd Floor, 2 Savoy Court
> The Strand
> London WC2R 0EZ
>
> Tel: 020 7240 2826
> Fax: 020 7240 2853

For Law Society advice and guidance on any area of practice, contact:

> Practice Advice Service
> The Law Society
> 113 Chancery Lane
> London WC2A 1PL
>
> Tel: 0870 606 2522
> Fax: 020 7316 5541
> DX: 56 London/Chancery Lane
> Email: lib-pas@lawsociety.org.uk

For enquiries about practice management generally, the information contained in this guide, or further information about Lexcel, contact:

> Lexcel Office
> The Law Society
> 113 Chancery Lane
> London WC2A 1PL
>
> Tel: 020 7320 5769
> Fax: 020 7316 5775

To join the Law Management Section of the Law Society, which comprises over 1300 managing and senior partners and practice managers, contact:

Law Management Section
The Law Society
113 Chancery Lane
London WC2A 1PL

Tel: 020 7316 5736
Website: www.lawsociety.org.uk

To obtain advice and guidance in any area of post-admission training, including management training, contact:

Continuing Professional Development Team
The Law Society
Ipsley Court
Redditch
Worcestershire B98 0TD

Tel: 0870 606 2500
Fax: 01527 500 018
Email: info.services@lawsociety.org.uk

For advice about complaints handling and setting up a complaints procedure, contact:

Office for the Supervision of Solicitors
Victoria Court
8 Dormer Place
Leamington Spa
Warwickshire CV32 5AE

Tel: 01926 820 082
Fax: 01926 431 435
DX: 292320 Leamington Spa 4

Introduction

How to use this guide

This *Solicitors' Guide to Good Management* divides management tasks into those related to 'Strategic Management' and those related to 'Operational Management'. This is consistent with the national Management Standards. Of course, not all lawyers are concerned with the strategic management of their practice, but many are asked to contribute to the development and implementation of strategies.

The guide is meant to be used as a management tool: a book to be consulted as required, rather than read from cover to cover. It breaks the management role down into simple, practical checklists. There is no magic involved, just clear and logical steps. You will, in fact, find this guide useful even if you believe that you have no management responsibilities of any kind. If you handle client matters you are advised to become familiar with Section 4.2 ('Case management') which starts on page 96. Also we all need to manage ourselves and our working relationships and to develop our skills. You are, in this regard, particularly referred to Section 5.1 ('Managing yourself') which begins on page 111.

The checklists tell you, the busy lawyer, what you need to do, often leaving you to decide how to go about the task in the context of your particular firm. This is an advantage because it allows you to tailor processes to the needs of your practice. The checklists can be used in a variety of ways, for example to help you to manage your time or your relations with your colleagues. They are concise and accurate but not necessarily comprehensive. First and foremost, they are meant to help you perform management tasks which are possibly not a part of your day-to-day activities. You should find checklists to cover all your management tasks, although they may not cover all your specialist activities. On page v you will find a full contents list and on page 193 an index. These will help you to find the checklist related to the management task you are contemplating.

Here are some examples of how you might use the checklists.

Addressing unfamiliar tasks

You may be faced with a task you have not performed for a long time, or perhaps never met before: recruiting a new member of staff, for example. How would you go about it? Alternatively, how can you check that someone else is performing the task correctly?

The contents pages tell you that in Chapter 3 ('Managing people'), Section 3.2 covers 'Personnel planning'. There are six checklists to help you. **'Planning human resource requirements'** will help you to check whether recruitment is the best option at this stage. **'Drawing up job descriptions'** will help you to clarify what the work entails, and who would be a suitable person to do it. **'Assessing and selecting people'** will give you guidance on how the right person should be chosen.

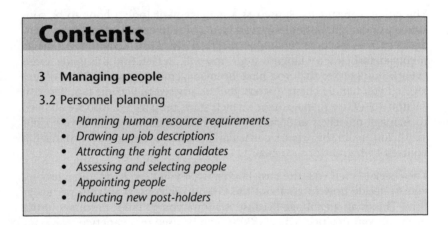

Contents

3   Managing people

3.2 Personnel planning

Tackling important tasks

You may have to do something critically important and you want to ensure you get it right: running an important meeting, for instance.

The index of keywords at the back of the book points you to the checklist for 'Leading meetings'. This will help you to ensure that you get the best from all participants, and reach well-informed decisions as rapidly as possible.

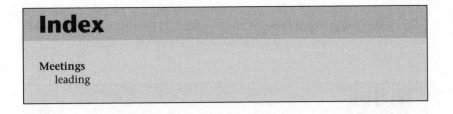

Checking that you are doing things properly

Preparing budgets for your team, department or practice may be something you do on a regular basis, but you may like to check occasionally that you are doing things properly.

The contents pages show there is a chapter on budgets under Chapter 6 ('Managing finance'), with a checklist specifically for '**Preparing budgets**'. There are also useful checklists to help you gain agreement to and monitor your budgets.

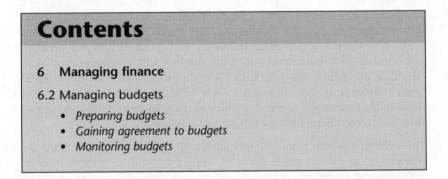

Carrying out a public task

Some aspects of management are more public than others, so it is important not only to get them right, but to be seen to be getting them right.

For example, '**Defining the practice's mission**' involves consultation and discussion with all those who have an interest in the success of your practice: not only with colleagues and personnel, but probably also with your bankers, and maybe even with key clients. The mission needs careful negotiation to ensure that it attracts the widest possible support.

Index

Mission
   Defining

Beyond this guide

Lawyers are subject to many professional rules as well as to the general law. For solicitors, these rules include not only the Solicitors' Practice Rules 1990 but also the Solicitors' Accounts Rules 1998 and the Solicitors' Investment Business Rules 1995. Many of these rules affect the way solicitors manage their practice. Practice Rule 15 (Costs Information and Client Care), for example, is a 'management rule' and decrees that solicitors shall give information about costs and other matters and operate a complaints handling procedure. Practice Rule 15 is supplemented by the Solicitors' Costs Information and Client Care Code 1999. The eighth edition of *The Guide to the Professional Conduct of Solicitors* (Law Society, 1999) contains all these rules, complemented by substantial guidance.

The current Practice Management Standards approved in July 2000 are reproduced in full on pages 177–190. They are the most complete set of management guidelines now available to solicitors, and set out management systems which practices should have in place. A template for such management systems, for adoption by practices, is provided by the *Lexcel Office Procedures Manual* (Moore and Dodd 2001).

Neither the Practice Management Standards, the *Lexcel Office Procedures Manual* nor the checklists contained in this publication, are intended to be a substitute for professional rules. However, practices are advised to establish systems and procedures as suggested by the Practice Management Standards and set out in the *Lexcel Office Procedures Manual*. Solicitors are advised to be guided in their management tasks by the checklists contained in this Guide as well as by the national Management Standards. Doing so will help practices and individual lawyers to comply with relevant professional rules.

Unless members of a practice have the knowledge and skills to understand and work effectively with the Practice Management Standards, the practice will not gain the maximum benefit from implementing them. The Law Society, therefore, wants to encourage individual solicitors to develop their own management skills, as well as to encourage practices to implement the Practice Management Standards and achieve certification under Lexcel. The publication of this guide is a further step towards this aim.

Part I

Strategic Management

What is strategic management?

The object of strategic management is to chart the direction of the practice and to ensure that it stays on course. Senior lawyers need to be excellent operational managers, but like senior managers in industry and other sectors, they also need to have the skills to develop and implement strategies to further their practice's mission. This mission may be expressed in different terms, such as a 'practice purpose statement'. The practice's strategy may, as suggested in the *Lexcel Office Procedures Manual* (Moore and Dodd 2001), be expressed as 'a plan for the future of the practice which identifies its main goals'. It may, as set out in the Practice Management Standards, be expressed as 'key objectives for 12 months and an outline strategy covering a further two years to provide a background against which a practice may review its performance'. How the strategy of your practice is expressed is less important than how it is developed. It is important to use a logical method to arrive at the best possible strategy and this guide will assist you to do that.

The senior partners and those reporting to them will devote much of their time to strategic management, as well as to fulfilling their legal and operational roles. Depending on the size and structure of the practice, relatively junior partners, fee-earners and non-qualified personnel may play an important part in strategic management.

Strategic management requires a sound understanding of the environment in which the practice is operating. To develop an appropriate strategy for the practice, you must be aware of what is happening in the world around you and seize opportunities to influence conditions in your favour. You need an objective view of the practice's strengths and weaknesses. You need to discover what are the opportunities for the practice and the threats facing it. A strategy should provide clear leadership and a vision for the practice. It is important to get all parties to agree on the practice's mission and its key objectives.

Once developed, defined, recorded and publicised, the practice's strategy and key objectives need to be achieved. This can be done by setting targets and developing and implementing relevant projects. The projects can be carried out by partners, fee-earners and non-qualified personnel. The project management process is set out in checklists contained in Section 5.3 'Project management' beginning on page 124. Those concerned with the implementation of such projects will need continual guidance and support to ensure that they are working in a way which is consistent with the practice's mission and key objectives.

The cycle of strategic management is continuous and complex with many loops and links. Once the strategy has been implemented, the performance of the practice against the mission and key objectives must be regularly measured and reviewed. This review will lead to the re-evaluation of the mission and key objectives and a consequent confirmation or amendment of the practice's strategy. The checklists on the following pages are designed to provide clear, practical guidelines for carrying out the tasks involved in the strategic management process.

1 Reviewing the environment

1.1 Reviewing the external environment
1.2 Reviewing the practice
1.3 Those with an interest in the practice – 'stakeholders'

2 Defining, implementing and reviewing the strategy

2.1 Defining the strategy
2.2 Implementing the strategy
2.3 Reviewing the strategy

1

Reviewing the environment

Reviewing the environment is about understanding the practice's strengths and weaknesses in the environment in which it is operating so that you can develop the most effective strategy. It involves:

1.1 Reviewing the external environment

This section is about identifying the opportunities and threats in the external environment in which you practise.

The checklists will help you to:

- develop cost-effective systems for reviewing the actual and potential client base;
- review and respond to the political and practising environments;
- identify the strengths and weaknesses of others, including competitors and associates.

The process of 'Reviewing the external environment' looks like this:

| Researching the actual and potential client base | 6 |

▼

| Reviewing the political and practising environment | 7 |

▼

| Identifying competitors and potential associates | 8 |

■ Researching the actual and potential client base

1 **Develop cost-effective systems for reviewing market possibilities** – choose cost-effective systems and techniques to identify opportunities to provide your services.

2 **Use external information** – get members of the practice and external contacts to provide relevant information on client needs.

3 **Use client feedback** – as an on-going process, interview your clients, face-to-face or over the telephone, and encourage them to tell you what they think about the practice's services and what they want in the future.

4 **Consider the use of structured feedback** – use formal interviews and questionnaires in appropriate circumstances.

5 **Get comprehensive market analyses** – make sure the information you have on the market possibilities for the practice's services is up-to-date, backed by good evidence and accurately reflects current and predicted trends.

6 **Take into account possible future interests and activities** – your market review must be forward-looking, taking into account the future interests and activities of the practice, associated organisations and competitors.

7 **Define your market as broadly as possible** – unless your practice has decided upon a niche strategy, do not take a narrow, traditional view: recognise opportunities for diversity and diversification, but at the same time do take care not to rush into a specialism in which the practice lacks expertise.

8 **Consider marketing by business sector rather than by a particular field of legal expertise** – if you have a number of clients in one business area, consider developing a sector team to provide the widest possible range of legal services to them and to potential new clients.

■ Reviewing the political and practising environment

1   **Develop cost-effective systems for gathering information** – choose systems and techniques which identify, in a cost-effective way, actual or potential opportunities and threats in the political, regulatory and practising environment.

2   **Use field intelligence** – get members of the practice and external contacts to provide relevant information on changes in the environment.

3   **Use feedback from clients and external contacts** – encourage clients and external contacts to discuss with you how they see the environment changing.

4   **Obtain comprehensive analyses of the environment** – make sure the information you have on the environment is up-to-date, backed by good evidence and accurately reflects current and predicted trends.

5   **Take into account possible future interests and activities** – your review of the environment must be forward-looking, taking into account the future interests and activities of the practice, its associates and competitors.

6   **Seize opportunities to change the external environment** – take the opportunities which present themselves to change the environment in your interests and to influence key opinion-formers and decision-takers.

7   **Use only fair and equitable methods to influence the environment** – make sure the methods you and the members of the practice use to influence the external environment are always ethical, consistent with the practice's values and sensitive to the values of all those who have an interest in the success of the practice.

8   **Be clear about the constraints imposed by the external environment** – understand what the constraints are and what their implications are for the practice.

■ Identifying competitors and potential associates

1 **Develop cost-effective systems for evaluating competitors and partners** – choose systems and techniques which identify, in a cost-effective manner, the strengths and weaknesses of existing and potential competitors and associates.

2 **Use field intelligence** – get members of the practice and external contacts to provide relevant information on competitors and potential associates.

3 **Use feedback from clients and external contacts** – encourage clients and external contacts to provide you with information on the activities of competitors and associates.

4 **Evaluate the strengths and weaknesses of your competitors and associates** – make sure your evaluation is based on up-to-date information and reflects current and predicted trends.

5 **Take into account possible future interests and activities** – your review should take account of the future interests and activities of the practice, its associates and competitors.

6 **Use fair and equitable methods** – make sure the methods you use to identify and evaluate competitors and associates are always ethical, consistent with the practice's values and sensitive to the values of all those who have an interest in the success of the practice.

7 **Adjust your plans** – amend your plans in the light of information on competitors and associates.

8 **Set comparative targets** – apart from your own internal targets, set targets which compare the practice's performance with that of its competitors.

9 **Consider any case for an association** – where an association with another practice or group of practices seems possible and advisable, develop a proposal which is backed by good evidence, acceptable in terms of the risk involved and consistent with the future plans of the practice.

1.2   Reviewing the practice

This section is about identifying the strengths and weaknesses of the practice.

The checklists will help you to:

- review the strengths and weaknesses of, and opportunities and threats to, your practice and the services you offer;
- look for ways of improving the practice's structures;
- identify the strengths and weaknesses of the practice team;
- review how you acquire and allocate financial resources.

The process of 'Reviewing the practice' looks like this:

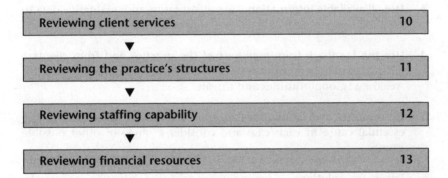

Reviewing client services	10

▼

Reviewing the practice's structures	11

▼

Reviewing staffing capability	12

▼

Reviewing financial resources	13

■ Reviewing client services

1   **Ask the three big strategic questions**:

- where is the practice now?
- where do we want it to go?
- how will we get there?

2   **Do a SWOT analysis of the practice** – analyse:

- strengths of the practice and how to capitalise on them;
- weaknesses within the practice and how to overcome or minimise them;
- opportunities available or anticipated which the practice could develop;
- threats to the practice's competitive position.

3   **Use all available information** – use quantitative and qualitative data to help identify strengths, weaknesses, opportunities and threats.

4   **Use the feedback from members of the practice and from clients** – encourage members of the practice and clients to discuss the strengths, weaknesses, opportunities and threats.

5   **Be rigorous and imaginative in your diagnosis** – try to get to the essential cause in each case and consider a range of other possible causes.

6   **Focus on solutions** – having diagnosed the situation accurately, consider how to improve services or the practice's operations.

7   **Decide upon your timing** – at least every six months, review the quality of client services.

■ Reviewing the practice's structures

1   **Identify obstacles and opportunities in organisational structure and communication systems** – look at the internal and external factors which may present obstacles or opportunities.

2   **Solicit suggestions** – encourage all members of the practice to suggest ways of improving structures and systems.

3   **Consult on proposed improvements** – consult those affected by changes to structures and systems in time for their views to be taken into account.

4   **Justify proposed improvements** – base your proposals for improvements on hard facts.

5   **Take into account the needs and expectations of all those who have an interest in the success of the practice** – discover their needs and expectations and modify proposals accordingly.

6   **Implement improvements in a timely manner** – make sure you take action in sufficient time to be able to meet the new circumstances.

7   **Communicate the practical requirements** – make sure all those affected know what they are required to do to implement the improvements and that they are committed to the change.

8   **Decide upon your timing** – do not review the practice's structures too frequently as continual organisational change can be unsettling and give rise to inefficiency.

■ Reviewing staffing capability

1   **Identify and evaluate the strengths and weaknesses of the staffing of the practice** – ensure your assessments are clear, unambiguous and fair.

2   **Base the assessments upon the best information available** – ensure, for example, that the review of staffing capabilities is based upon the practice's personnel appraisal system.

3   **Choose appropriate techniques** – select identification and evaluation techniques which meet your information needs.

4   **Acknowledge the potential of lawyers and personnel from diverse backgrounds and experience** – develop a mix of different skills and experience in the team.

5   **Present a balanced view** – where weaknesses are identified, present these in a balanced way, so that you also take into account strengths and potential.

6   **Share your findings with the management team** – share your evaluation of the capability of the practice's staff with management team members, paying due regard to personal feelings and issues of confidentiality.

7   **Carry out the assessments in time** – make sure the assessments are available in time to support decisions on the structure and development of the staff of the practice.

8   **Consider the future** – when reviewing the capability of the staff, consider both current and future circumstances and needs.

9   **Decide upon the timing and regularity** – review the staffing capability of the practice regularly but not too frequently, say, every year.

■ Reviewing financial resources

1   **Develop systems to collect information** – you need information from those inside and outside the practice who are responsible for acquiring and allocating financial resources.

2   **Know who your friends are** – know as much as you can about all those who can either help or hinder the process of acquiring funds.

3   **Judge your performance in context** – when selecting criteria for judging the performance of the practice in acquiring and allocating funds, take into account the context and character of its organisation.

4   **Use commonly accepted performance measures** – use commonly accepted measures which allow you to compare the performance of the practice with others.

5   **Make comparisons** – compare the performance of the practice and its constituent units with other similar practices.

6   **Look at alternative means of financing** – compare your current performance with alternative means of acquisition and allocation of financial resources over the short, medium and long terms.

7   **Take contingency action** – where your review reveals threats or opportunities, identify, communicate and implement alternative feasible courses of action.

1.3 Those with an interest in the practice – 'stakeholders'

This section is about identifying the interests of all those who have a stake in the success of your practice and getting them on your side.

'Stakeholders', as well as having a specific meaning in law, is a management term. For management purposes, it means all those who have an interest or 'stake' in the success of the practice. They need to be carefully defined. For most practices, they would normally include not only the partners themselves, but also the other fee-earners and non-qualified personnel, as well as bankers and key clients. Depending on the practice's circumstances, they could include more remote groups such as associate and correspondent practices, frequently used counsel and important suppliers, such as retained firms of accountants.

It is important to define who your stakeholders are, to define their interests and to consult them in the course of the decision-making process. However, remember that this should not be used as a method of avoiding taking responsibility for a decision.

The checklists will help you to:

- be clear about the interests of various groups of stakeholders;
- develop a good relationship with your stakeholders;
- secure their support and assistance in the development of the practice's strategy.

This section covers:

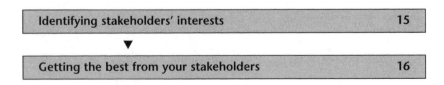

| Identifying stakeholders' interests | 15 |

▼

| Getting the best from your stakeholders | 16 |

■ Identifying stakeholders' interests

1   **Be realistic and comprehensive when identifying stakeholders' interests** – and take account of current and likely future activities of the practice.

2   **Use a wide range of methods to identify stakeholders' interests** – employ both quantitative and qualitative techniques.

3   **Consult widely with people throughout the practice** – use both formal and informal methods.

4   **Use only fair and equitable methods** – be even-handed and ensure that the methods used are sensitive to social and economic diversity.

5   **Develop a relationship of trust with stakeholders** – consult stakeholders in a way which generates their trust and leads to open expression of their interests.

6   **Take account of stakeholders' interests** – modify your plans appropriately but do not forget that it is your responsibility to take the decision and to get it right.

7   **Take advantage of opportunities stakeholders provide** – show how stakeholders can help your practice to achieve its plans.

8   **Acknowledge and resolve differences** – where stakeholders' interests appear to be based on a misunderstanding or are at variance with the practice's proposed mission and key objectives, acknowledge these differences and try to resolve them.

9   **Monitor and evaluate stakeholder reaction** – where an action is likely to excite particular or exceptional stakeholder interest, establish a way of monitoring and evaluating the reaction.

■ Getting the best from your stakeholders

1   **Evaluate your stakeholders** – evaluate stakeholders' capabilities to help or hinder the achievement of the practice's objectives.

2   **Make your evaluation comprehensive** – consider all stakeholders and their interests in relation to current and likely future activities of the practice.

3   **Influence your stakeholders** – encourage them to act in favour of the practice.

4   **Communicate regularly with stakeholders** – this will maximise their support.

5   **Secure collaboration and support wherever possible** – ask them to make this support public.

6   **Take action to remove the possibility of stakeholders hindering the achievement of the practice's objectives** – where stakeholders' interests are at variance with the practice's proposed mission and key objectives, discuss ways of resolving these differences.

7   **Learn from experience** – use your experience to help you manage stakeholder relationships in the future.

2

Defining, implementing and reviewing the strategy

Defining, implementing and reviewing the strategy is about deciding upon the mission and key objectives of the practice, putting them into effect and reviewing their achievement or otherwise with a view, if necessary, to amending them for the future.

It involves:

2.1 Defining the strategy

This section is about developing and adopting a mission statement, values and key objectives for the practice and gaining support for the strategy that these encapsulate.

The checklists will help you to:

- develop, define and obtain agreement to your practice's mission, values and key objectives;
- gain support for these from all those with an interest in your practice.

The process of 'Defining the strategy' looks like this:

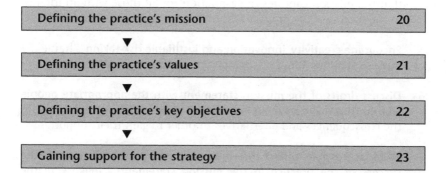

Defining the practice's mission	20
Defining the practice's values	21
Defining the practice's key objectives	22
Gaining support for the strategy	23

■ Defining the practice's mission

1 **Consult all those who have a stake in the practice** – consult all those individuals, groups and organisations (including partners, other members of the practice, key clients, bankers, associate organisations and suppliers) who have an interest in the practice to gain their views and suggestions.

2 **Base the mission statement upon your review of client services** – see that the mission statement reflects, in particular, the strengths and weaknesses of your practice and any opportunities and threats revealed by a review of client services.

3 **Describe the practice's role and ethos** – try to capture, in the mission statement, the ethos of the practice and its role in the environment.

4 **Make the mission statement both challenging and realistic** – check that the mission captures the aspirations of all those with an interest in the success of the practice and that these aspirations are achievable.

5 **Encourage creativity, innovation and justifiable risk-taking** – frame the mission statement in a way which encourages innovative activity.

6 **Discuss drafts of the mission statement with the appropriate people among those who have an interest in the practice's success** – explain the consequences and alternatives in order to gain their support.

7 **So far as possible, reflect the views of all who have an interest in the success of the practice in the mission statement** – make sure the mission attracts the widest possible spectrum of support.

8 **Provide a vision for the future** – frame the mission statement within an overall vision of the position of the practice in the future.

9 **Review the mission statement regularly** – update the mission in response to trends and opportunities.

10 **Keep the mission statement short** – a very few paragraphs, perhaps only a single paragraph, will normally suffice to encapsulate the practice's mission.

11 **Publish the mission statement** – it will help all members of the practice to focus their contribution creatively.

■ Defining the practice's values

1   Consult all who have an interest in the success of the practice on the formulation of values – incorporate their needs and ideas where possible.

2   **Be consistent** – make sure the practice's values are consistent with its mission.

3   **Be realistic** – make sure the practice's values can be reflected in day-to-day practice and in working relationships.

4   **Include guidance on dealing with difficult situations** – particularly how to respond when under pressure or when interests are in conflict.

5   **Be clear yet flexible** – make sure the practice's values are unambiguous yet allow people to respond and adhere to them in different ways.

6   **Be comprehensive** – make sure the practice's values cover all aspects of your operations, clients and suppliers.

7   **Keep up-to-date** – check regularly to ensure your values are up-to-date and allow for likely future circumstances and issues.

8   **Consider publishing** – there is much to be gained in understanding and commitment if the mission and values of the practice are made known to all those who have an interest in the success of the practice.

■ Defining the practice's key objectives

1 **Be consistent** – make sure that the practice's key objectives are consistent with mission and values.

2 **Deliver the mission** – make sure that the key objectives are capable of delivering the practice's mission within an acceptable timescale and at an acceptable cost.

3 **Be specific** – include sufficient detail to allow the development of specific programmes, projects and operating plans.

4 **Cover the essential** – include key objectives concerning information technology, the services you wish to offer, the client groups to be served, how services are to be provided and the way in which services are designed to meet client needs.

5 **Provide a framework for decisions** – the key objectives should facilitate decisions about, for example, capital expenditure, office location and staffing.

6 **Address issues relating to the services of the practice** – these may include physical access to the premises, languages spoken, facilities for clients, electronic communication, etc.

7 **Acknowledge constraints** – clearly acknowledge and express any constraints upon objectives.

8 **Define achievable and measurable key objectives** – and state the types of measures and criteria to be used.

9 **Consult all interested parties** – hold open and realistic discussions over the objectives.

10 **Revise key objectives** – to take advantage of any actual or anticipated changes in circumstances.

■ Gaining support for the strategy

1 **Consult and negotiate openly** – ensure that the mission, values and key objectives are influenced by, and consistent with, the considerations of all interested parties.

2 **Find the best balance of interests** – where interested parties are in conflict, find realistic and rational compromises which balance the interests and acknowledge the tensions.

3 **Enlist the support of those with an interest in the success of the practice** – present the mission, values and key objectives to them in such a way as to attract their support.

4 **Minimise any problems arising from lack of support** – where less than full support is achieved, identify the consequences and take action to minimise any problems.

5 **Maintain regular consultation** – communicate regularly to ensure support is available when needed.

2.2 Implementing the strategy

This section is about implementing the strategy once the mission statement, values and key objectives for the practice have been adopted.

The checklists will help you to:

- fix the targets necessary to achieve the strategy;
- develop projects to realise the strategy and meet those targets;
- secure the resources necessary to realise the strategy and
- develop measures and criteria to assess whether or not the practice is on course to meet its key objectives.

Note that the project management process itself is set out in a number of checklists in Section 5.3 'Project management', beginning on page 124.

The process of 'Implementing the strategy' looks like this:

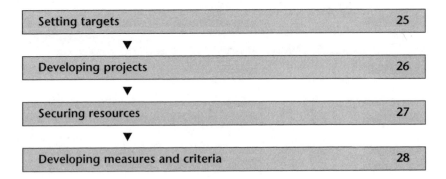

Setting targets	25
Developing projects	26
Securing resources	27
Developing measures and criteria	28

■ Setting targets

1 **Agree upon clear targets** – only have targets which are realistic, necessary, unambiguous and explicit, by setting 'SMART' targets:

   Specific   – precise about what must be achieved;

   Measurable – able to be seen to have been achieved;

   Agreed   – accepted by all involved;

   Realistic   – achievable;

   Time-bound – to be completed by a specified time.

2 **Agree upon targets with those responsible** – and, where appropriate, amend targets with those responsible for meeting them.

3 **Take into account all relevant considerations** – when agreeing upon targets take into account the capabilities of the people concerned, the systems to be used and the circumstances which apply.

4 **Make your targets consistent** – check that your targets are designed to achieve the mission and key objectives of your practice.

5 **Check the implications for other parts of the practice** – where targets need to be revised, identify the implications for other parts of the practice and communicate these to the relevant people.

6 **Gain commitment** – agree upon and promote targets in ways which encourage commitment and creative thinking.

7 **Agree upon deadlines** – for each target obtain agreement with the people concerned upon the date for the achievement of specific progress towards the target.

■ Developing projects

1   **Settle the project scope** – clarify the scope of the project with all concerned and ensure that its object is to help achieve the practice's strategy, meet its key objectives and achieve its targets.

2   **Check that the project is viable** – are its goals realistic within the time and resources allowed for the project?

3   **Estimate and obtain agreement to the cost of the project** – include in the calculation all costs including the human and physical resources and overheads, and allow for inflation if the project is to last for more than a year.

4   **Settle the project budget** – obtain agreement on the budget and how payments and reimbursements will be made.

5   **Agree upon a management structure for the project** – settle how the work is going to be broken down, who will be responsible for what and what reports will be made with what frequency. If fee-earners are to be involved in the project, make appropriate amendments to billing targets.

6   **Break down the work into manageable work packages** – and allocate responsibility for each work package and settle with those responsible the methods they will use to deliver the work and their level of autonomy.

7   **Settle a base plan with all concerned** – make sure that everyone involved agrees to working to and reporting against the baseline project plan.

8   **Agree upon the quality and success criteria** – define the specific quality to which the project must be delivered and agree how successful completion will be measured.

■ Securing resources

1 **Generate support and secure resources for projects** – communicate the benefits to those who control the resources.

2 **Make a clear, unambiguous, consistent and supportable case** – present valid information in an appropriate format.

3 **Be ethical and consistent** – ensure your activities to obtain support are ethical and consistent with the values of the practice.

4 **Respect the views of all those with an interest in the success of the practice** – demonstrate how these are consistent with projects.

5 **Avoid undue risks** – avoid unacceptably hazardous relationships and potential damage to the good name of the practice.

6 **Exploit alliances and trade-offs** – use contacts and relationships and be prepared to compromise as long as this does not risk producing negative consequences for the practice.

7 **Show commitment and drive** – in the way you present your case, reflect the commitment and drive of those who will be using the resources.

■ Developing measures and criteria

1 **Develop techniques to evaluate the practice's performance** – develop measures and criteria to evaluate the achievement of the practice's mission and key objectives.

2 **Select appropriate measures and criteria** – make sure they are appropriate to the nature and character of the mission and key objectives.

3 **Use cost-effective measures and criteria** – make optimum use of existing sources of data and means of data gathering.

4 **Get timely information** – choose measures and criteria which will provide you with information in time for you to respond effectively.

5 **Get sufficient information to be able to make judgements** – choose measures and criteria which will give you sufficient information to make judgements about progress towards the key objectives.

6 **Take into account the views of all those with an interest in the success of the practice** – include their differing perspectives in your measures and criteria.

2.3 Reviewing the strategy

This section is about evaluating your practice's achievement of its mission and key objectives once they have been implemented with a view to amending them, if necessary, for the future.

The check lists will help you to:

- identify whether the practice has succeeded or failed to meet its key objectives and targets;
- evaluate the causes;
- review your practice's performance against its key objectives and targets;
- reconsider the mission and key objectives of the practice in the light of the findings.

The process of 'Reviewing the strategy' looks like this:

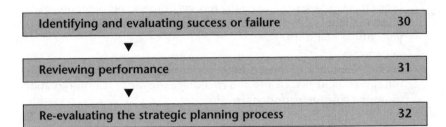

Identifying and evaluating success or failure	30
▼	
Reviewing performance	31
▼	
Re-evaluating the strategic planning process	32

■ Identifying and evaluating success or failure

1 **Look for the causes of success or failure** – find out why the key objectives and targets are, or are not, being achieved.

2 **Provide evidence** – support your explanations of the causes of success or failure with facts.

3 **Evaluate your explanations** – estimate how likely it is that these are the real causes.

4 **Explain your preferences** – where there are alternative explanations, report these and state the reason for your preference.

5 **Present your arguments logically and comprehensively** – and summarise the arguments in ways to suit different audiences.

6 **Prepare for objections** – where it is difficult to find a remedy for a cause, prepare your arguments to counter possible objections.

7 **Learn from experience** – draw the lessons from success or failure, make these available to those who could learn from them, and use them in your future planning.

8 **Provide feedback to those whose performance is examined** – explain the causes identified clearly and encourage the use of this information to improve future performance.

■ Reviewing performance

1   Measure the performance of the practice against defined criteria – and, in particular, consider to what extent the practice's mission statement, key objectives and targets are being achieved.

2   Consider all the evidence – look at both defined criteria and planned measurements but include informal sources of information.

3   Reach conclusions based on clear criteria – support these conclusions with facts.

4   Provide a rounded picture of the practice's performance – describe it in relation to the mission and key objectives.

5   Discuss possible reasons for failure – where performance fails to meet the agreed criteria, suggest possible reasons and discuss these, as appropriate, with those who have an interest in the success of the practice.

6   Consult with interested parties – before the publication of any report on performance consult as appropriate with those who may be affected.

7   Be fair and equitable – make sure that the review is even-handed, realistic and without favour to any groups or individuals.

8   Propose improvements – do not hesitate to bring forward any ideas to improve the performance of the practice that arise in the course of the review and seek suggestions from others.

■ Re-evaluating the strategic planning process

1   **Reconsider the practice's mission and key objectives** – at least every three years, carry out a review of the strengths and weaknesses of the practice, the opportunities available to it and the threats facing it, in the light of its current mission and key objectives.

2   **Ask the three big strategic questions once again** – in the light of the current situation, ask whether you are satisfied about where the practice is, whether you want it to go anywhere and, if so, how you can help it get there?

3   **Look at current trends in the external environment** – consider whether changes in the external environment might have affected the current appropriateness of the mission and key objectives of the practice.

4   **Consider the client services, structure, management capability and financial resources of the practice** – take a view whether these support the current mission and key objectives of the practice or if they or the mission and key objectives need to be changed.

5   **Consider the performance of the practice** – take the opportunity to review any evaluation of performance and achievement that may have been carried out during the period.

6   **Consult with stakeholders** – take the views of those who have an interest in the success of the practice about whether the practice still has the right mission and key objectives.

7   **Reconsider the values of the practice** – in the light of these considerations and consultations, review whether it would be appropriate to amend the values of the practice.

8   **Provide a realistic and comprehensive analysis** – support any proposals you may make to reformulate the strategy or to change the organisation of the practice with clear evidence.

Part II

Operational Management

What is operational management?

You will note that the first checklists in this section are about managing yourself. As a lawyer, you are central to the management process even if you have no specific role in running the practice. Whatever else you do, you need to communicate with clients, colleagues and staff, manage your limited time and perhaps delegate a heavy workload. Throughout your career, you will need to develop both your legal and your management skills. The checklists in Section 3.1 'Managing yourself' starting on page 39 are designed to help you to do all this effectively.

The key purpose of management is the achievement of the practice's objectives and the improvement of its performance. Operational management is the process of attaining the defined key objectives of your practice, or those of your team, by using available resources to the best effect.

Operational management involves managing the practice, or your part of it, as effectively as possible; being clear about what you are expected to achieve; and designing systems and procedures which take account of your objectives. You need continuously to seek and implement ways of providing a service of improved quality.

Management means getting things done through people. You have to make sure you have the right people. You have to develop a team and help each member of the team develop the skills needed to perform the work effectively. You need to plan the work and allocate it among the team, setting individual objectives and providing feedback on performance. Managing people involves building effective working relationships and dealing with problems, being careful to be fair and even-handed in all your dealings.

As a lawyer with management responsibilities, you may need to ensure that the practice has a system in place which will provide enough financial information to manage it effectively. You may often be required to prepare budgets for the expenditure, and perhaps the fee income, for your part of the practice. It may be your responsibility to ensure that these financial targets are met and that all members of the practice, including non-qualified personnel, are aware of how they can help in improving the practice's financial performance. Operational management also involves obtaining and using information to aid decision-making and leading and participating effectively in meetings. Above all, effective communication is an important key to being a capable operational manager.

The Practice Management Standards, reproduced in full on pages 177–190, cover many aspects of operational management in the sections concerning Management Structure, Financial Management, Managing People, Office Administration and Case Management.

Any person, whether a solicitor or not, having responsibility for the operational management of a practice should be guided by the Practice Management Standards, supplemented by the *Lexcel Office Procedures Manual*. Any solicitor thinking of starting up, or taking responsibility for the management of a small practice should, in addition, consult *Setting Up and Managing a Small Practice* (Smith 1995).

Operational management is complex and requires, for success, a range of skills and knowledge, together with disciplined time management. All operational management decisions should flow from the mission and key objectives. The checklists in this book provide some simple, practical guidelines for tackling management tasks effectively. You will find them relevant whether you are a partner, a fee-earner or a non-qualified member of the practice. If you are not a partner, you may find your role is to contribute to rather than to take full responsibility for an activity.

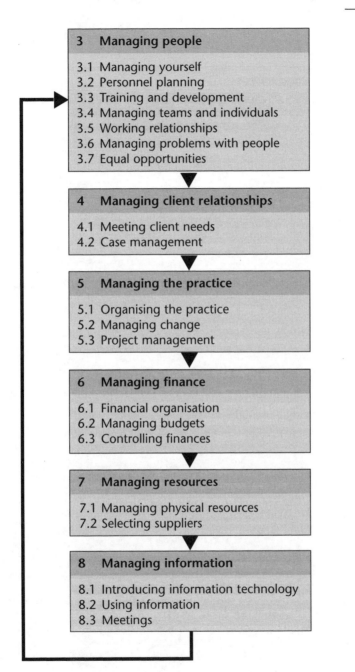

3   Managing people

3.1 Managing yourself
3.2 Personnel planning
3.3 Training and development
3.4 Managing teams and individuals
3.5 Working relationships
3.6 Managing problems with people
3.7 Equal opportunities

4   Managing client relationships

4.1 Meeting client needs
4.2 Case management

5   Managing the practice

5.1 Organising the practice
5.2 Managing change
5.3 Project management

6   Managing finance

6.1 Financial organisation
6.2 Managing budgets
6.3 Controlling finances

7   Managing resources

7.1 Managing physical resources
7.2 Selecting suppliers

8   Managing information

8.1 Introducing information technology
8.2 Using information
8.3 Meetings

3

Managing people

Managing people is about meeting client requirements with and through people. It involves:

3.1 Managing yourself

This section is about making the most efficient use of your time, knowledge and skills.

The checklists will help you to:

- communicate effectively with clients, colleagues, and staff;
- be clear about your objectives and priorities;
- plan your time and allow for contingencies;
- delegate work where appropriate;
- be decisive;
- develop the skills you need to meet your objectives.

The process for 'Managing yourself' looks like this:

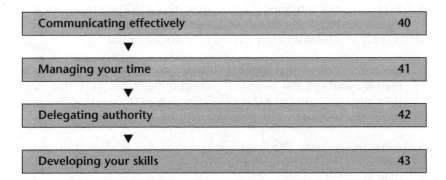

Communicating effectively	40
Managing your time	41
Delegating authority	42
Developing your skills	43

■ Communicating effectively

1 **Never presume that a message has been understood** – test everyone's perception of a situation frequently:

 - when delegating, ask for instructions to be repeated;
 - when taking instructions from a client, repeat them in the course of the interview and at the end;
 - confirm all oral understandings in writing. *

2 **Avoid memo and e-mail wars** – if you are angry, never send a letter, memo or e-mail to relieve your feelings; wait until you feel calmer and then talk about the matter with the person concerned.

3 **Avoid writing self-indulgent letters** – these are the letters which give you more satisfaction than they give to the recipient (they almost always start with the word 'I'); write to confirm rather than to surprise and, above all, never send a bill which comes as a shock to your client.

4 **Keep everyone informed** – spend some time deciding to whom you should send copies of each communication, and remember that information which informs one person may irritate another.

5 **Never tell a client that a matter is going to be easy** – to do so may massage your ego and reassure the client initially, but when things, as they often do, turn out to be more complicated than at first foreseen, you will immediately lose your client's trust.

6 **Avoid unnecessary deadlines** – if you miss a self-imposed deadline, your client will be disappointed; give yourself more time and be earlier than expected.

7 **Ask for advice as frequently as you give it** – temper your advice in the form of a question; even tough advice can be made more palatable if you seek your client's own advice and agreement.

8 **Give bad news face-to-face** – we all have to break bad news; never put things in writing until you have spoken.

9 **Remember to say thank you** – the easiest way to motivate people is to thank them. Of course, you must mean what you say – hypocrisy is easily recognised. Always remember that you yourself do not like to be taken for granted – neither does anyone else.

■ Managing your time

1   **Be clear about your objectives** – be clear about what you have to achieve when and what the priorities are.

2   **Identify what needs to be done to achieve these objectives** – identify what you and others need to do to achieve your objectives and estimate how long each activity will take.

3   **Plan your time** – plan how to fit activities into your time on an annual, monthly, weekly and daily basis to ensure objectives are achieved on time; include time for evaluation and break down large tasks into smaller components.

4   **Delegate** – review your activities and, where possible, delegate those activities which could be done by one of your team, with training and guidance where appropriate.

5   **Handle paper once only** – when dealing with paper, decide immediately to respond, refer, file or destroy.

6   **Take decisions** – when faced with a choice, either make your choice or decide what further information you need to be able to make an informed choice.

7   **Control interruptions** – make it clear when you welcome consultation with others, and when you require uninterrupted time to complete an activity.

8   **Control digressions** – keep your objectives in mind and do not indulge in digressions nor allow others to do so.

9   **Allow for contingencies** – allow time in your planning for additional activities or for activities to overrun.

10 **Review your activities** – review your progress on a regular basis and reschedule activities as necessary.

■ Delegating authority

1 **Delegate responsibility and authority to competent personnel** – only delegate to those capable of doing what is asked of them, but remember that people develop by being stretched.

2 **Do not delegate accountability to the client** – accept final responsibility even if, internally, you are not responsible for any error.

3 **Delegate, do not dump** – do not delegate jobs which you find difficult or irksome just for that reason.

4 **Never presume that a message has been understood** – when delegating any task, ask for your instructions to be repeated and confirm all oral understandings in writing.

5 **Be prepared to provide support where needed** – encourage people to ask for support when required.

6 **Delegate explicitly** – be clear and unambiguous about what is delegated and to whom.

7 **Delegate in time** – allow sufficient time for the action to be carried out.

8 **Gain commitment** – delegate in a way which ensures understanding and inspires commitment and enthusiasm.

9 **Agree the details** – agree with those concerned the way in which the responsibilities will be carried out and the resources available.

10 **Provide sufficient resources** – make sure sufficient resources are readily available.

11 **Provide opportunities** – so far as possible provide equal opportunities to take on responsibilities to all members of the practice.

12 **Review delegation** – keep delegation under review and revise as necessary.

■ Developing your skills

1   **Take responsibility for developing yourself** – ensure you develop the skills you need to achieve your objectives.

2   **Identify your own strengths and weaknesses** – measure your current skills as a manager against appropriate standards, and by getting feedback from your senior and other colleagues and from members of your team.

3   **Set yourself clear development and training objectives** – make your objectives achievable, realistic and challenging.

4   **Consider both your needs and those of the practice** – include objectives which will develop you as a member of the practice and of a team, balancing the practice's needs against your own.

5   **Allow sufficient time and resources** – allocate sufficient time and appropriate resources to achieve your development objectives.

6   **Review progress and performance on a regular basis** – check your progress against your objectives with your senior colleagues and specialists at regular intervals, perhaps twice a year, and revise your plan as appropriate.

7   **Compare feedback with your own perceptions of your performance** – compare the views of your senior and other colleagues, and the members of your team with your own assessment, and attempt to improve your future performance as a result.

3.2 Personnel planning

This section is about making sure that you have the right people to provide the practice's services to its clients.

The checklists will help you to:

- be clear about the people who are needed to meet the practice's objectives;
- specify the skills, qualities and attributes you are looking for;
- attract the right candidates;
- assess the candidates against specific criteria and select those most appropriate;
- make appointments and draw up contracts of employment;
- prepare and implement induction programmes;
- develop plans to re-deploy people;
- make redundant people who are no longer required.

The process of 'Personnel planning' looks like this:

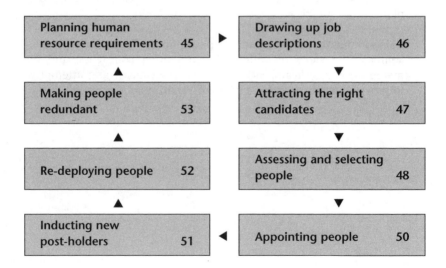

■ Planning human resource requirements

1 **Identify the human resources required to achieve the mission of the practice** – the practice will need people to achieve its mission and key objectives.

2 **Prepare a personnel plan** – this will help ensure that skills, knowledge and experience within the practice are developed to meet needs indicated in the practice's mission statement and key objectives.

3 **Base your plan on current, valid and reliable information** – check that your information is sound and up to date.

4 **Support your plan with appropriate calculations** – estimates of the human resources required will need to be supported by calculations of the time required to complete tasks and the associated personnel costs, including training and development, and provision for special needs.

5 **Identify the skills and personal qualities required of the team and individuals** – look for a balance of strengths within the team.

6 **Be clear about the practice's organisational constraints** – specify where financial considerations, internal policy or legal constraints affect plans.

7 **Consult colleagues and members of your team** – take into account the views of your colleagues, specialists and your team on how best to meet future human resource requirements.

8 **Present plans on time and with the appropriate level of detail** – make sure that plans are accurate, contain sufficient detail for a decision to be made and are presented in time for the practice to take the necessary action.

■ Drawing up job descriptions

1   **Prepare written job descriptions** – document the skills, knowledge and experience required of fee-earners and other staff, and the tasks they are required to perform in the form of a written job description but see that employment contracts reserve job flexibility where appropriate.

2   **Be clear about the role** – state the purpose of the work clearly and how it relates to the practice's key objectives and to those of your team.

3   **Specify the position in sufficient detail** – think carefully about the title, reporting relationships, key objectives and responsibilities and the terms and conditions of service.

4   **Specify the type of person required** – be clear about the qualifications, knowledge, experience, competence and qualities he or she will need.

5   **Consult colleagues and members of your team** – take into account the views of your colleagues, specialists and your team on the definition of the position and the skills, knowledge and qualities required.

6   **Check that the specification is clear and concise, and complies with the practice's requirements** – consult specialists if you are in doubt.

7   **Agree the job description with appropriate people** – check and agree the specification with colleagues, specialists and your team before taking any action to recruit or to transfer or change a person's position.

8   **Review job descriptions regularly** – keep specifications under review, at least yearly, to ensure that they still describe the work and meet the practice's needs.

■ Attracting the right candidates

1 **Follow documented procedures** – follow the procedures and guidelines for recruitment that the practice has adopted.

2 **Consult colleagues** – ask colleagues for their advice and opinions on how and where you should recruit.

3 **Publicise the position** – let people know that the practice is recruiting and the sort of person needed.

4 **Select appropriate media** – the job description will help to decide the best way of advertising the position by selecting from a range of appropriate media, including:

- local press, specialised legal press or national press;
- local radio;
- job centres, recruitment agencies or head hunters;
- staff newsletters and notice boards;
- friends and colleagues (word of mouth);
- direct approaches to possible candidates.

5 **Draw up the advertisement** – this should include job title, indication of salary, type of contract (permanent, temporary, full or part-time), where the position is based, information about your practice, brief description of the job, type of person required, how to apply, to whom to apply, closing date and the address to apply to.

6 **Comply with legal requirements** – make sure you comply with employment laws particularly those referring to unfair discrimination, which cover recruitment.

7 **Attract sufficient applicants** – see that there are a sufficient number of suitably qualified applicants to allow a good choice.

■ Assessing and selecting people

1   **Document the practice's procedures** – the practice should have documented arrangements which evaluate the skills, knowledge and experienced possessed by applicants for posts in the practice, and their integrity and suitability.

2   **Obtain, or draw up, criteria against which to judge candidates** – have clear, measurable criteria. For example, send applicants a copy of the job description and a form to complete; the contents of the completed application may then be checked against the requirements of the job description; questions at interviews may be related to the completed application and to the job description.

3   **Get sufficient information from candidates to be able to make a decision** – use a variety of appropriate assessment techniques, such as CVs, application forms, interviews, tests and references to ensure you get all relevant information.

4   **Check all information concerning the candidate** – take up references, check with the Office for the Supervision of Solicitors concerning any complaints and make bankruptcy and credit rating searches for positions of trust.

5   **Judge the information obtained against specified selection criteria** – you should be able to defend your decision to accept or reject a candidate: judge candidates against the selection criteria and do not let irrelevant factors affect your decision.

6   **Be fair and consistent** – correct any deviations from agreed procedures before you make your selection.

7   **Maintain confidentiality** – tell only authorised people of your selection recommendations.

8   **Keep clear, accurate and complete records** – you may need to refer back to them.

9   **Keep candidates informed** – tell candidates promptly and accurately of decisions following each stage of the selection process.

10 **Check that the choice is justifiable** – make sure you have selected the most suitable candidate; if in doubt, consult colleagues or specialists.

11 **Review the process and make appropriate recommendations for improvement** – consider every aspect of the process on a regular basis, perhaps yearly, and make any recommendations for improving it, so that you and your colleagues can achieve a better result in the future.

■ Appointing people

1 **Confirm all details** – check that you have the necessary information and that your selection process has complied with the practice's procedures and with the law.

2 **Settle the appointment with relevant people** – check that those involved in the selection process, personnel specialists and senior management agree with the appointment.

3 **Make a clear job offer** – even if you offer the position face to face or by telephone, follow up with a letter, including job title, salary, holiday and pension entitlement, other benefit terms and conditions, start date and place and reporting relationship; make it clear if the offer is subject to satisfactory references or medical report.

4 **Take up references** – write to or telephone referees; ask specific questions to confirm the information about the new post-holder and to allay any doubts you may have.

5 **Confirm the appointment** – or withdraw the offer if references or the medical report are unsatisfactory.

6 **Provide a written contract of employment** – settle and sign a contract of employment within three months of the date of employment.

7 **Prepare the work space** – make sure that the new post-holder has a suitable work space with all the equipment required to be productive.

8 **Prepare an induction programme** – prepare a programme to introduce the new post-holder to colleagues in the practice and to gain the essential knowledge and skills to be productive.

9 **Inform colleagues** – let people know about the arrival of the new post-holder, the post-holder's role and the reporting arrangements; ask colleagues to make the new arrival welcome.

■ Inducting new post-holders

1   **Establish a documented induction process** – the practice should have documented arrangements to provide an induction process for new post-holders.

2   **Welcome the new post-holder** – make yourself available to welcome people on arrival if possible.

3   **Provide an induction programme for each new post-holder** – this may include:

- information about the practice;
- introductions to colleagues;
- introductions to the work environment, instructions about the job and briefings about work procedures;
- meetings with specialists;
- background reading to gain useful knowledge about the job;
- training in skills and techniques specific to the practice;
- training in skills and knowledge identified as lacking through the selection process.

4   **Assign a mentor or adviser** – ask an experienced member of the practice to be available to provide advice and information to the new post-holder and generally to make the post-holder feel welcome.

5   **Monitor the induction programme** – book times in your diary to check that all is going well.

6   **Evaluate the induction programme** – check that it has been completed successfully and settle any further development required.

7   **Get feedback** – ask the new post-holder for an initial impression of the practice, colleagues and the induction programme; make recommendations for improvement as appropriate.

■ Re-deploying people

1 **Keep people informed about current procedures** – ensure that members of the practice are aware of any re-deployment procedures, including appeals procedures.

2 **Consult** – consult with individual members of the practice and with their representatives over any possible re-deployment. This will improve co-operation and may result in alternative, more cost-effective approaches being adopted.

3 **Seek advice** – seek advice from specialists on all aspects of re-deployment in order to comply with legal and organisational requirements.

4 **Settle clear and fair selection criteria** – settle criteria for selecting those to be re-deployed that are unambiguous, can be clearly applied, are fair and comply with legal and organisational requirements.

5 **Apply selection criteria fairly and consistently** – consult with specialists if you are in doubt.

6 **Make a clear re-deployment offer** – although you will probably make the offer face-to-face, support this with a letter specifying the new post, its location, the reporting relationship, any changes in salary, benefits or other terms and conditions, and any relocation allowances; make it clear what the options are if the offer is not accepted.

7 **Allow time** – allow a reasonable time to consider the offer, taking into account the individual's personal circumstances as well as the urgency for the practice.

8 **Provide help and support** – do this in order to enable those re-deployed to become productive in their new roles and situations as quickly as possible.

9 **Keep people informed** – tell colleagues and other members of the practice about the re-deployment and the reason, without breaching confidentiality.

10 **Recommend any changes to policy or procedures** – tell the appropriate people of ways in which the practice's procedures could be improved.

■ Making people redundant

1   **Keep members of the practice informed about current procedures** – ensure that personnel are aware of redundancy procedures, including appeals procedures.

2   **Avoid redundancies which are not economically justified** – accurate personnel planning will minimise the need for redundancies, but where these are inevitable, explore alternatives such as early retirement or part-time working.

3   **Consult** – consult both members of the practice and their representatives about the redundancy plan; consultation will improve co-operation and may result in alternative, more acceptable approaches being adopted.

4   **Seek advice** – seek advice from specialists on all aspects of making people redundant in order to ensure you comply with legal and organisational requirements.

5   **Settle clear and fair selection criteria** – settle selection criteria that are unambiguous, can be clearly applied, are fair and comply with legal and organisational requirements.

6   **Apply selection criteria fairly and consistently** – consult specialists if you are in doubt.

7   **Prepare to break the news** – rehearse what you will say to the people who will be made redundant, including responses to likely questions.

8   **Break the news quickly and compassionately** – tell people face-to-face, quickly, clearly, confidentially and compassionately that they will be made redundant and what help is available to them.

9   **Offer alternative work** – where there is other suitable work available, offer this with details of terms and conditions.

10 **Offer counselling** – offer the individuals concerned appropriate counselling, resources, training and time off work to help them to find another position and to cope with the personal and practical implications of redundancy.

11 **Keep relevant people informed** – tell colleagues and other members of the practice about the redundancies and the reasons for them.

12 Recommend any changes to policy or procedures – tell the appropriate people of ways in which the practice's policy or procedures could be improved.

3.3 Training and development

This section is about making sure that the members of the practice have the knowledge and skills to do their work.

The checklists will help you to:

- introduce a training and development programme;
- develop a balanced team with all the knowledge and skills required;
- help individuals identify and develop the skills they need;
- coach or guide individuals to help them develop new skills;
- assess the performance of members of the practice against training and development objectives;
- evaluate and improve the training and development process.

The process for 'Training and development' looks like this:

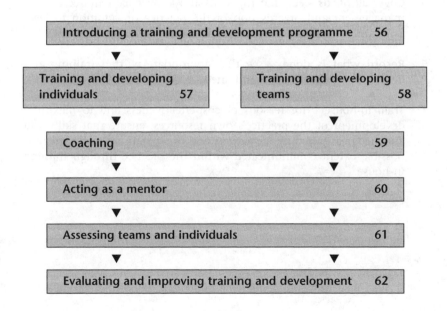

■ Introducing a training and development programme

1   **Set a policy** – the practice should have a policy to maximise the job satisfaction and performance levels of all personnel through the provision of appropriate training.

2   **Document training arrangements** – introduce documented training and development arrangements and make them available to be consulted by members of the practice.

3   **Set objectives** – include in the objectives that all partners, principals, and staff are trained and developed to a level of competence appropriate to their work.

4   **Assess needs** – normally as part of a performance appraisal, ensure that training and development needs are assessed for each person in the practice against the key objectives of the practice and are reviewed at least annually.

5   **Cover all needs** – see that the skills and knowledge required for the management and organisation of the practice (in addition to legal skills and knowledge) are provided in training and development.

6   **Record what is done** – see that appropriate written training and development records are maintained.

7   **Train in-house** – for reasons of cost-effectiveness and to maximise development of the practice's own resources, ensure that skills and knowledge acquired by fee-earners and other staff are to the greatest possible extent communicated within the practice through training in-house.

■ Training and developing individuals

1   **Involve individuals in identifying their own training and development needs** – get them to identify their own strengths and weaknesses.

2   **Discuss training and development needs and plans with individuals** – gain individuals' commitment by involving people in planning how they should meet their needs.

3   **Be clear about the objectives of training and development plans** – your objectives should be clear, relevant and realistic for the individual.

4   **Balance the practice's needs with the aspirations of the individual** – plans should help individuals to develop the skills they need in their current position and to meet future work requirements and career aspirations.

5   **Optimise the use of resources** – when planning training and development activities, use available resources effectively.

6   **Review your plans regularly** – on a regular basis, perhaps every quarter, discuss and agree improvements to training and development plans with the individuals concerned, other colleagues and specialists.

7   **Provide equal opportunity** – provide equal access to training and development activities to all individuals.

8   **Monitor individual training and development** – provide coaching or act as a mentor where necessary.

■ Training and developing teams

1   **Involve all team members in identifying the team's training and devel-opment needs** – get them involved in identifying their own strengths and weaknesses.

2   **Identify the team's strengths and weaknesses** – look at each individual and at the team as a whole and acknowledge the team's strengths and weaknesses to carry out current and future work.

3   **Consult all team members on how to meet training and development needs** – gain the team's commitment by involving them in planning how to meet their needs.

4   **Prioritise** – where the resources are not sufficient to meet all training and development needs, decide which needs must be addressed in order to meet the key objectives of the practice.

5   **Be clear about the objectives of training and development plans** – your objectives should be clear, relevant and realistic for individuals and the team as a whole.

6   **Optimise the use of resources** – when planning training and develop-ment activities, use available resources effectively.

7   **Provide equal opportunity** – provide equal access to training and development activities to all team members.

8   **Minimise unproductive friction** – be clear about each individual's responsibilities in the team to minimise the risk of bad feeling.

9   **Review your plans regularly** – discuss and agree improvements to training and development plans with team members, other colleagues and specialists, at appropriate intervals.

■ Coaching

1   **Identify the individual's training and development needs** – use appropriate methods to assess the learning needs of the person you are coaching.

2   **Agree learning objectives** – discuss and reach agreement with the individual about the level of skills to be achieved.

3   **Analyse the components of skills** – make sure that you understand the different components of the skills and the sequence in which they need to be learnt.

4   **Agree upon the steps to be taken** – decide with the individual what steps needs to be taken to achieve the desired objectives.

5   **Take account of the individual** – design your coaching to match the individual's learning preferences, and deliver the coaching in an appropriate manner and at a suitable pace.

6   **Identify inhibiting factors** – identify clearly and discuss with the individual any factors which are inhibiting the learning process.

7   **Check progress** – check on progress regularly and modify the coaching as appropriate.

8   **Receive feedback** – ask individuals how they feel about the process, and their speed of progress, and modify the coaching as appropriate.

9   **Give feedback** – provide, in a positive and encouraging manner, timely feedback on learning progress.

■ Acting as a mentor

1 **Identify the individual's learning needs** – discuss and identify what needs to be learned with the individual to be provided with guidance and with others involved.

2 **Agree upon the support that individuals require** – specify and agree the roles, responsibilities and resources needed to help the individual achieve their learning objectives.

3 **Identify and overcome any difficulties in obtaining this support** – identify likely difficulties in obtaining the necessary people and resources, and settle ways of overcoming these difficulties.

4 **Develop effective working relationships** – both with the individual and with others who can provide support.

5 **Provide guidance** – provide accurate, timely and appropriate advice and guidance on learning methods and opportunities, and on other sources of information and advice.

6 **Encourage independent decision-making** – provide guidance in a way which encourages individuals to take responsibility for their own development and enables them to make informed decisions.

7 **Facilitate learning and assessment opportunities** – identify and facilitate opportunities for individuals to develop, practise, apply and assess new skills, knowledge and experience in a structured way.

8 **Provide continuing support** – within the agreed role, provide individuals with support for their learning, development and assessment, as required.

9 **Give feedback** – provide timely feedback to individuals on their progress, in a positive and encouraging manner.

10 **Review the process** – at appropriate intervals, discuss the learning process and your relationship with those being provided with guidance, and modify as appropriate.

■ Assessing teams and individuals

1   **Be clear about the purpose of the assessment** – do not confuse an assessment of the results of training and development with an individual 'performance appraisal' (for performance appraisal guidance see Section 3.4 'Managing teams and individuals'). Note, however, that an assessment of the results of an individual's training and development is a legitimate, and even essential, part of a performance appraisal.

2   **Get people involved** – give team members the opportunity to contribute to their own and their team's assessment of their training and development.

3   **Provide equal opportunity** – provide equal access to the assessment to all team members.

4   **Develop objective criteria** – develop and settle clear criteria for the assessment of training and development programmes that are consistent with the practice's key objectives.

5   **Use appropriate assessment methods** – these may include the testing of knowledge and skills, observation of performance at work, contributions from other team members and appraisal discussions.

6   **Make assessment decisions against the criteria** – base your decisions on matching the information you obtain from the assessment process against the settled criteria.

7   **Give feedback** – provide teams and individuals with feedback on the assessment of training and development in a positive and encouraging manner.

8   **Make regular assessments** – see that the outcome of the training and development of each person in the practice, and of each team, are assessed against the key objectives of the practice at least annually.

9   **Maintain confidentiality** – tell only authorised people of the results of the assessment.

■ Evaluating and improving training and development

1   **Identify clearly the training and development objectives** – be clear about what the objectives are and how you will assess the practice's or your team's success in achieving them.

2   **Debrief those involved** – discuss with the individuals and teams involved in training and development how useful the training and development programme was, how satisfied they were with its delivery and how relevant it is to their work.

3   **Identify the impact of the training and development** – evaluate the benefits compared with costs and the negative impact if people had not been trained and developed.

4   **Check whether objectives have been achieved** – apply the measures agreed to assess to what extent objectives have been achieved.

5   **Find suitable alternatives where training and development did not meet the needs** – discuss with the individuals and teams involved and reach agreement with them concerning any, more appropriate, training and development plans.

6   **Modify team and individual training and development plans** – where plans were unrealistic, discuss the plans with the teams and individuals involved and agree to modify them.

7   **Pass on your experience** – discuss the strengths and weaknesses of the training and development processes used with specialists and your senior and other colleagues, so that they can gain from your experience.

8   **Benefit from your experience** – use your experience of training and development processes to help identify more appropriate programmes in the future.

3.4   Managing teams and individuals

This section is about making sure that the practice gets the work done.

The checklists will help you to:

- encourage and maintain a productive work environment;
- set objectives and appraise performance;
- plan the work to meet your objectives;
- allocate work amongst your team;
- give advice and support;
- champion activities;
- provide feedback.

The process for 'Managing teams and individuals' looks like this:

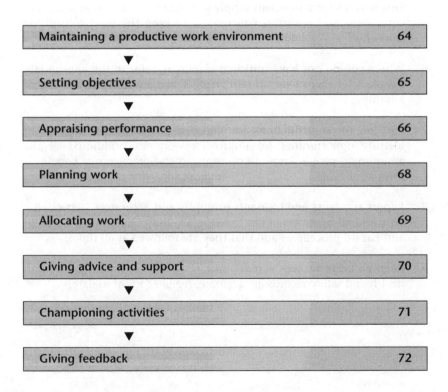

Maintaining a productive work environment	64

▼

Setting objectives	65

▼

Appraising performance	66

▼

Planning work	68

▼

Allocating work	69

▼

Giving advice and support	70

▼

Championing activities	71

▼

Giving feedback	72

■ Maintaining a productive work environment

1   **Ensure the environment is as conducive to work as possible** – involve all members of the practice or your team in assessing the work environment to see if there are different ways it could be arranged to improve productivity.

2   **Ensure that conditions satisfy legal and organisational requirements** – check the relevant legislation and your internal health and safety procedures, and make sure you have a safe work environment.

3   **Cater for special needs** – provide for any special needs of members of the practice to ensure they can work productively.

4   **Make sure equipment is properly maintained and used only by competent personnel** – regularly check all equipment to see that it is properly maintained and that relevant personnel have been trained to use it.

5   **Ensure you have a sufficient supply of resources** – plan what materials, equipment and resources you require to keep the practice running smoothly.

6   **Where you do not have sufficient resources, refer to the appropriate people** – let them know immediately if you are likely to run out of anything.

7   **Pass on recommendations for improving conditions** – where you identify opportunities for improving working conditions, let the appropriate people know right away, so the practice can benefit as soon as possible.

8   **Report accidents and incidents promptly and accurately** – check that you, and all members of the practice, are fully aware of the accident and hazard procedures and that they are followed at all times.

9   **Keep accurate records** – make sure the practice's maintenance and health and safety records are accurate, legible and up to date.

■ Setting objectives

1 **Document the procedures** – your practice should have documented arrangements to record the responsibilities and objectives of each partner, principal, and member of staff.

2 **Involve personnel in setting their objectives** – ask members of the practice to be proactive in identifying the objectives.

3 Set clear objectives – agree to set 'SMART' objectives which are:

Specific	– precise about what must be achieved;
Measurable	– able to be seen to have been achieved;
Agreed	– accepted by all involved;
Realistic	– challenging but achievable;
Time-bound	– to be completed by a specified time.

4 **Explain objectives clearly** – when explaining objectives, think about the person to whom you are talking, and make sure you communicate in a manner and at a pace which is appropriate.

5 **Encourage personnel to seek clarification** – check on the individual's understanding and provide opportunities for putting questions.

6 **Update objectives regularly** – review objectives as often as appropriate, but at least every year, in the light of changes in individual and team workloads and in the practice's key objectives.

7 **Check that objectives have been achieved** – as part of the process of setting objectives, agree upon a date for reviewing whether or not the objectives have been achieved.

8 **Provide feedback** – do this both formally and informally and include constructive suggestions and encouragement for improving future performance.

■ Appraising performance

1 **Document the procedures** – your practice should have documented arrangements to evaluate the performance of each partner, principal and member of staff at least annually against their defined and documented responsibilities and objectives. The arrangements should provide for a record in writing of the performance appraisal, to be kept confidential to the practice and the post-holder.

2 **Be clear about the purpose of the appraisal** – the purpose could be:

- to check that objectives have been achieved;
- to check the quality of work and that client requirements have been met;
- to appraise performance of teams as well as individuals;
- to recognise competent performance and achievement;
- to decide upon bonuses or other financial rewards.

3 **Get people involved** – give individuals the opportunity to evaluate their own and their team's performance and allow them to discuss their potential, motivation, development needs, and their views concerning the practice and its procedures.

4 **Provide equal opportunity** – when appraising the performance of a team, provide equal access to performance appraisal to all team members.

5 **Evaluate performance** – assess actual performance against the measures agreed when setting objectives, taking into account any changes of circumstances.

6 **Make appraisal decisions** – decide how well teams and individuals have performed: whether they met their objectives, whether there were mitigating circumstances, and the individual contributions they have made to the success of the practice.

7 **Move from appraisal to objective setting** – do not remain backward-looking; move from pure appraisal of previous objectives to a consideration of whether these are still appropriate in current circumstances and whether they should be amended; objective-setting and appraisal are a continuum.

8   **Share the appraisal decisions** – allow individuals, and even teams, to say how far they agree with your decision.

9   **Keep clear and accurate records** – remember that you may have to refer back to performance appraisals.

10   **Maintain confidentiality** – tell only authorised people of the results of performance appraisals.

■ Planning work

1 **Plan work in order to meet the practice's key objectives** – make sure that your plans are consistent with the objectives of your team and the practice as a whole.

2 **Assess the degree of direction required by each member of the team** – inexperienced or less confident people may need far more direction and help in planning their work than their more experienced and self-assured colleagues.

3 **Encourage individuals to contribute to the planning of work activities and methods** – the people who will be carrying out the work are likely to have sound ideas as to the most efficient ways of doing it.

4 **Include the suggestions of members of the team on working methods, resources and time required** – this will help to ensure commitment to the work.

5 **Select work methods and activities which meet both operational and developmental objectives** – choose work methods and activities which balance management priorities, the practice's key objectives, legal requirements and opportunities for individual development.

6 **Select cost-effective work methods** – choose work methods which make the best use of available material, finance and people.

7 **Seek advice where legal requirements and organisational or developmental objectives conflict** – consult your senior colleagues, specialists and external advisers.

■ Allocating work

1   **Allocate work according to the availability of resources and skills** – to meet the practice's key objectives, optimise the resources and the skills of the personnel available.

2   **Define team and individual responsibilities and limits of authority** – make sure people understand their responsibilities and the limits of their authority, and the responsibilities and authority of those with whom they work closely in order to avoid possible conflict, duplication or omission of important responsibilities.

3   **Provide learning and developmental opportunities within the work allocated** – take opportunities to develop new skills which the personnel involved will need in the future.

4   **Brief people on their work in a manner and at a level and pace which is appropriate** – the inexperienced or less confident may need a more detailed briefing on their responsibilities and work than their more experienced and self-assured colleagues.

5   **Encourage people to seek clarification** – check on their understanding and give them opportunities to ask questions.

6   **Provide access to those who can help them meet their objectives** – people may need access to senior or other colleagues, specialists and external advisers to help them meet their work and developmental objectives.

7   **Provide the right level of supervision** – some people will require much closer supervision than others.

8   **Ensure that work allocations are realistic** – carefully calculate the time, cost and importance of the work to ensure appropriate resources have been allocated.

9   **Re-allocate work where appropriate** – if the way work was allocated proves to be unrealistic, or the practice's demands change, re-allocate work whilst minimising any detrimental impact on time or cost.

10 **Benefit from your experience** – evaluate how well you have allocated work in order to improve your performance in the future.

■ Giving advice and support

1   **Provide advice and support to members of the practice and your team** – help them to solve problems and maintain progress.

2   **Be timely** – provide advice only when necessary; do not interfere without just cause; provide the advice only when requested or when it will improve the quality of work.

3   **Distinguish opinion from advice** – make it clear when you are offering a personal opinion or preference rather than professional advice.

4   **Give evidence** – support your advice with facts.

5   **Be sensitive** – when providing advice and support recognise the personal needs and positions of those to whom you are offering it.

6   **Provide advice and support** in ways that:

   ■ confirm joint commitment to objectives;
   ■ demonstrate trust in those carrying out the work;
   ■ give encouragement and reinforce confidence.

7   **Enable people to work autonomously** – only provide the advice and support necessary to allow them to make progress, then withdraw.

■ Championing activities

1   **Promote benefits** – promote the benefits of projects to all those with an interest in the success of the practice.

2   **Identify threats** – identify threats to projects at an early stage.

3   **Counter threats** – where you can anticipate threats, take steps to counter them in the planning and delegation of work.

4   **Consider the reasons and sources of threats** – take into account the reasons and sources of the threats in planning how to counter them.

5   **Give clear support** – make your support apparent to those under threat and keep them regularly informed about the situation.

■ Giving feedback

1   **Seek opportunities to provide feedback on performance to both teams and individuals** – feedback helps people to understand if they are doing a good job or if there are areas in which they can improve. Feedback can be given formally or informally, orally or in writing. Do not limit feedback to formal performance appraisal sessions.

2   **Choose an appropriate time and place to give the feedback** – feedback is more useful and relevant if provided quickly. It is often appropriate to give positive feedback publicly, but a quiet word in private is usually the best way to give negative feedback.

3   **Recognise good performance and achievement** – take opportunities to congratulate people on their successes.

4   **Provide constructive suggestions and encouragement for improving future performance** – when people are not performing well, tell them, and advise them how they can improve.

5   **Encourage people to contribute to their own assessment** – ask open-ended questions about how they view their performance and invite them to be specific.

6   **Provide feedback in sufficient detail and in a manner and at a level and pace which is appropriate to those concerned** – some may readily understand your feedback on their performance, while with others it may be necessary to be very specific about their performance and what improvements are required.

7   **Encourage people to seek clarification** – check their understanding and give them the opportunity to ask questions.

8   **Encourage people to make suggestions on how systems and pro-cedures could be improved** – individual performance may be greatly enhanced by changes to procedures and working practices.

9   **Record details of any action agreed** – make a note of agreements reached to maintain or improve performance or change procedures, and inform the appropriate people.

10 **Review performance** – check back at an appropriate point to see whether performance has improved or has been maintained.

3.5 Working relationships

This section is about building effective working relationships.

Solicitors are required by their function to be critical. Perhaps because of this, many of us tend to be negative in our dealings with other people. This section will encourage you to give positive messages first and negative messages afterwards and in a constructive manner.

The checklists will help you to:

■ encourage collaboration between everyone in the practice;
■ promote the practice's values;
■ take time to build effective working relationships;
■ consult colleagues and keep them informed;
■ be honest and open with people;
■ provide support and keep your promises;
■ take steps to minimise any possible conflicts.

The process of building effective 'Working relationships' looks like this:

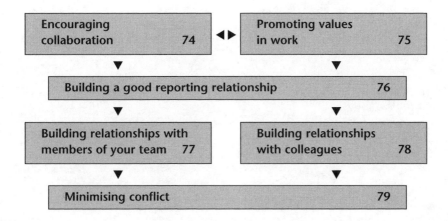

■ Encouraging collaboration

1 **Explore collaborative and consultative working arrangements** – set these up where projects would benefit from them.

2 **Provide adequate resources** – provide the resources to allow collaborative and consultative working arrangements to succeed.

3 **Induct and train new members of the practice** – help them to understand the ways of working, backgrounds and expectations of their fellows to achieve the practice's mission and key objectives.

4 **Be consistent** – ensure that values and key objectives are consistent across the practice.

5 **Provide support** – where difficulties in collaboration and consultation occur, provide support to help members of the practice to find ways to resolve them, consistent with the practice's requirements.

■ Promoting values in work

1 **Consult and provide guidance** – be clear on the ways in which the practice's values are to be expressed in work and in working relationships.

2 **Consult members of the practice and other persons with an interest in its success** – consultation will help you gather ideas, suggestions and feedback on the ways in which values are expressed in work and in working relationships, as well as gaining commitment to those values.

3 **Publish guidance on the practice's values** – publish guidance to inform, explain and define the limits of acceptable practice.

4 **Use appropriate means of consultation and guidance** – the means must suit the circumstances, degree of urgency and the likely reaction of the audience.

5 **Be consistent** – make sure the means of consultation and guidance are consistent with the policies and procedures of the practice.

6 **Commit to overcoming problems** – where problems occur which cannot be resolved in the normal way, be prepared to allocate additional resources towards investigating and resolving them, or take disciplinary action where appropriate.

■ Building a good reporting relationship

1 **Keep the person to whom you report informed** – provide an appropriate level of detail about activities, progress, results and achievements. Consider providing a regular, perhaps monthly, short 'highlight' report.

2 **Provide information about emerging opportunities or threats** – let the person to whom you report know about possible opportunities and threats accurately and with the appropriate level of urgency.

3 **Seek information and advice** – ask for information and advice on policy and ways of working whenever appropriate.

4 **Present clear proposals for action** – present proposals at the appropriate time and with the right level of detail. The greater the degree of change, expenditure or risk involved in your proposal, the greater will be the detail required – but preface any lengthy proposal with a short executive summary.

5 **Identify the reasons for the rejection of a proposal** – try to find out the reasons for the rejection of a proposal and, if appropriate, put forward alternative proposals.

6 **Make efforts to maintain a good relationship with the person to whom you report** – even if you do have disagreements, try to prevent these damaging your relationship.

7 **Meet your objectives** – always try to fulfil the objectives agreed upon; where circumstances have prevented you from meeting objectives, inform the person to whom you are reporting as soon as possible.

8 **Support the person to whom you report** – give your backing, especially in situations which involve people outside your team.

9 **Be open and direct** – discuss any concerns about the relationship directly and, if possible, face-to-face.

■ Building relationships with members of your team

1   **Take time to build honest and constructive relationships** – get to know your team, and allow them to get to know you.

2   **Keep your team informed** – provide them with relevant information on the practice's mission, values and key objectives.

3   **Consult about proposed activities** – give the members of your team the opportunity to state their views so these can be taken into account.

4   **Encourage your team to offer their ideas and views** – use 'open' questions to elicit their contributions.

5   **Give people recognition for their ideas and views** – thank them and show you value their ideas.

6   **When suggestions are not taken up explain the reasons clearly** – where it is not possible to take up a good idea, acknowledge the value of the idea and explain why it is not possible to adopt it.

7   **Encourage people to seek clarification** – check their understanding and provide them with an opportunity to ask questions.

8   **Keep your promises** – when you make promises and undertakings to your team, make sure they are realistic and that you honour them.

9   **Support your team** – give your backing, especially in situations which involve people outside your team.

10 **Be open and direct** – discuss concerns about the quality of work directly with the relevant member of the team.

■ Building relationships with colleagues

1   Take time to build honest and constructive relationships with colleagues – get to know your colleagues and allow them to get to know you.

2   Encourage open, honest and friendly behaviour – ask 'open' questions to get their opinions.

3   Share information and opinions with colleagues – identify those who could benefit from any information or idea you have and those whose views could be of value to you.

4   Offer help and advice with sensitivity – you can often help a colleague or provide advice on a difficult problem.

5   Deal courteously with colleagues when you have differences of opinion – you will not always agree with colleagues: discuss these different opinions respectfully and try to understand their views.

6   Resolve conflicts amicably – always maintain mutual respect.

7   Keep your promises – when you make promises to colleagues, make sure they are realistic and that you honour your commitment.

■ Minimising conflict

1 **Explain the standards of work and behaviour you expect** – some people will readily appreciate the standards required; others may need a fuller and more detailed explanation.

2 **Allocate work and responsibilities** – you can greatly reduce the potential for conflict by making sure your team is clear about the responsibilities of each member.

3 **Encourage people to discuss problems which affect their work** – make it clear that you are available to help resolve these problems.

4 **Identify potential or actual conflicts quickly** – when conflicts appear, or are likely to do so, involve the relevant individuals in identifying the nature and cause of the conflict early on.

5 **Take prompt action to resolve conflicts** – do not let conflicts fester, but take decisive action to deal with them.

6 **Ensure solutions satisfy legal and organisational requirements** – check that you are not infringing any legislation or procedures and that your solution helps meet the practice's objectives.

7 **Keep accurate and complete records of any conflict** – particularly where the conflict is serious, keep notes of what happened and what was agreed, in case there is any comeback.

8 **Monitor the situation** – keep an eye on the situation to ensure that the conflict does not re-emerge.

9 **Learn from your experience** – use the experience to help you and your team to avoid conflicts or resolve them speedily in the future.

3.6 Managing problems with people

This section is about ensuring the best outcome when you have problems with those for whom you are responsible.

The checklists will help you to:

- counsel people when personal matters are affecting their work;
- implement grievance and disciplinary procedures;
- dismiss people, where this is the most appropriate option.

The section 'Managing problems with people' covers:

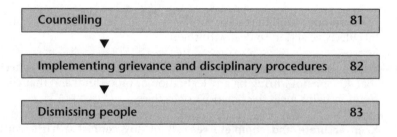

| Counselling | 81 |

▼

| Implementing grievance and disciplinary procedures | 82 |

▼

| Dismissing people | 83 |

■ Counselling

1   **Identify the need for counselling quickly** – changes in mood, a fall-off in performance, stress symptoms, or a word from a colleague may indicate the need to provide counsel to individuals.

2   **Consider whether counselling is appropriate in the circumstances** – if the situation is very serious counselling might preclude disciplinary action; therefore, consider consulting with a human relations specialist before proceeding with counselling.

3   **Choose an appropriate time and place** – counselling on personal matters affecting an individual's work, needs to take place in a private place and at a time which allows for full discussion without interruptions.

4   **Follow the practice's guidelines or personnel policies** – check to make sure you follow the practice's procedures.

5   **Encourage the individual to discuss the situation fully** – help the individual to understand the situation and all the relevant factors.

6   **Encourage the individual to take responsibility for his or her own decisions and actions** – remember you are helping someone to solve a problem, not solving it for them.

7   **Recommend a counselling service where appropriate** – if you do not have the skills or knowledge to help the individual, recommend a specialist in the practice or an external professional service.

8   **Monitor the situation** – keep an eye on the situation and offer further counselling sessions if these are necessary.

9   **Maintain confidentiality** – keep all documents confidential and only discuss the situation with authorised people.

■ Implementing grievance and disciplinary procedures

1   **Keep people informed about current procedures** – make sure that personnel have up-to-date copies of the practice's grievance and disciplinary procedures, and remind them of these from time to time.

2   **Implement grievance and disciplinary procedures with a minimum of delay** – act promptly to prevent the situation getting out of hand and causing damage to the practice or to the people concerned.

3   **Act in accordance with legal and organisational requirements** – check both the legal situation and the practice's procedures, if necessary with a specialist.

4   **Ask for advice** – where appropriate, ask a specialist, a senior or other colleague for confidential advice on how to deal effectively with difficult situations, especially where legal and organisational requirements conflict.

5   **Involve a third party** – where appropriate, ask a third party – specialist, superior or other colleague – to become involved to ensure you implement the procedures fairly and impartially.

6   **Be, and be seen to be, impartial** – get all the facts of the case – it may be advisable to obtain a written statement from each person involved; make decisions that are objective and can be shown to be free of personal bias.

7   **Keep accurate and complete records** – make detailed notes of the whole episode and, where appropriate, without breaching confidentiality, copy these to the members of the practice concerned and to specialists.

8   **Monitor the situation** – keep an eye on the situation and ensure that the problems which triggered the grievance or disciplinary procedure do not reappear.

9   **Learn from your experience** – use the experience to help you, and the members of the practice, to avoid the problems or to resolve them quickly in the future.

10 **Recommend any improvements to the procedures** – tell the appropriate people of any ways in which the procedures could be improved.

■ Dismissing people

1   **Avoid the need to dismiss people** – good recruitment and selection, training, development and counselling techniques will minimise the need for dismissals.

2   **Follow disciplinary procedures** – make sure you follow the practice's disciplinary procedures in detail.

3   **Seek advice** – seek advice from colleagues and specialists, inside or outside the practice, on all aspects of dismissals in order to ensure you comply with legal and organisational requirements.

4   **Involve a third party** – it is normally appropriate to ask a third party – specialist, senior or other colleague – to become involved in order to ensure you follow procedures fairly and impartially.

5   **Get the facts** – make sure you get all information relevant to the dismissal. If necessary, suspend the member of the practice on full pay until you have all the facts available.

6   **Prepare to break the news** – rehearse what you will say to the member of the practice, including responses to likely questions, and enlist the support of colleagues or specialists as appropriate.

7   **Give clear, fair grounds for dismissal** – check that your grounds for dismissing the person are clear and fair, and give these both orally and in writing.

8   **Summarily dismiss individuals in the case of gross misconduct** – dismiss people without notice, or pay in lieu of notice, in the event of gross misconduct. When in doubt, suspend on full pay until you can consult specialists or gather all the facts.

9   **Cordon off the incident** – it is often wise to ensure that a dismissed employee leaves the office immediately, to avoid other members of the practice being unsettled.

10   **Keep personnel and colleagues informed** – tell members of the practice and colleagues about the dismissal and the reasons for it, without breaching confidentiality.

11   **Review the procedures and reasons for dismissal** – tell the appropriate people of any ways in which the procedures could be improved or future dismissals avoided.

3.7 Equal opportunities

This section is about providing equal working opportunities, encouraging diversity and avoiding unfair discrimination.

The checklists will help you to:

- develop, implement and evaluate the practice's equal opportunities commitment;
- encourage people to use a range of appropriate working styles;
- promote fair working practices.

The process of managing 'Equal opportunities' looks like this:

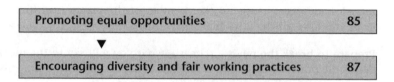

| Promoting equal opportunities | 85 |

▼

| Encouraging diversity and fair working practices | 87 |

■ Promoting equal opportunities

1   **Document procedures** – practices should have documented arrangements on equality of opportunity including recruitment and employment and they should have regard to guidance on equality of opportunity issued by the Law Society from time to time. The practice's policy should ensure equal treatment regardless of sex, marital status, race, religion, colour, nationality, ethnic or national origins, or disability.

2   **Keep yourself informed of developments in the field of equal opportunities so that you can contribute to the development of the practice's equal opportunities policy** – offer your views and recommendations on how the policy should be developed.

3   **Involve members of the practice, colleagues and clients** – encourage them to help develop your equal opportunities action plan, identify areas where opportunities are unfairly restricted and gain their commitment to the plan.

4   **Agree measures** – specify the criteria by which you can assess progress in your action plan.

5   **Collect and analyse information** – find out whether certain members of the practice, or potential members, are denied access to development, employment or promotion opportunities.

6   **Identify the strengths of all members of the practice** – review underrepresented groups, and identify how their strengths could contribute to the practice.

7   **Identify special needs** – identify the special needs of members of the practice.

8   **Publish your action plan** – include in it plans to meet special needs and address any imbalances and to take positive action to support underrepresented groups.

9   **Communicate the action plan to all members of the practice** – make sure that all are aware of their responsibilities and duties within the equal opportunities policy and action plan.

10 **Provide training and development opportunities** – provide appropriate training and development to help personnel fulfil their duty to implement the action plan.

11 **Implement the action plan and evaluate performance** – use agreed measures to monitor the practice's progress in the implementation of the action plan and modify the plan as appropriate.

■ Encouraging diversity and fair working practices

1   **Communicate the equal opportunities policy to all members of the practice** – make sure that everyone is aware of the standards of behaviour expected, and of the consequences of unacceptable behaviour.

2   **Encourage a diversity of working styles** – encourage all members of the practice to develop a repertoire of appropriate working styles.

3   **Support natural working styles and behaviour** – encourage all members of the practice to use their natural and preferred working style and behaviour as long as these are consistent with the achievement of the practice's objectives.

4   **Discourage stereotyping** – discourage members of the practice from imposing stereotypes and styles of working which are inconsistent with individuals' natural and preferred working styles.

5   **Discourage rigid approaches** – where particular styles of working are inhibited without good work-related reasons, provide feedback and suggestions to encourage more diverse approaches.

6   **Give feedback and suggestions sensitively** – where the style of working is impeding the achievement of objectives, give feedback and suggestions to individuals in ways which are sensitive to their racial, social, gender or physical circumstances.

7   **Challenge discriminatory behaviour** – clearly explain the problems discriminatory behaviour may cause, and the sanctions which will be applied if it continues.

8   **Implement disciplinary procedures** – take prompt action where unfair discriminatory behaviour persists.

9   **Seek guidance and support** – where you are unsure of the effect on another person of your own behaviour or that of a member of your team or of a colleague, seek guidance and support from specialists, inside or outside the practice.

4

Managing client relationships

Managing client relationships involves:

4.1 Meeting client needs

Excellent client service and positive client–solicitor relationships are keys to the success of a practice. This section is about maintaining an effective operation to meet client needs.

The checklists will help you to:

- be clear about the needs of your clients;
- plan to meet those needs;
- design your operational systems to meet client specifications;
- assure a quality service.

The process of 'Meeting client needs' looks like this:

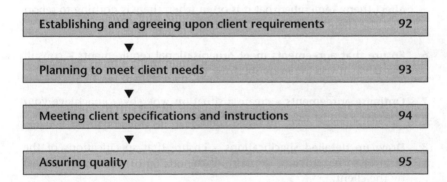

| Establishing and agreeing upon client requirements | 92 |

▼

| Planning to meet client needs | 93 |

▼

| Meeting client specifications and instructions | 94 |

▼

| Assuring quality | 95 |

■ Establishing and agreeing upon client requirements

1   **Research your clients' needs** – use formal and informal techniques to identify the services your clients, or potential clients, need.

2   **Design your services to meet your clients' needs** – ensure your services meet organisational requirements and resource constraints.

3   **Describe your services clearly** – explain your services to clients, think about the person you are talking to, and make sure you communicate in a manner and at a pace which is appropriate.

4   **Understand the true objectives of the client** – draw out from the client the full extent of his or her needs; never merely process the instructions you receive.

5   **Communicate frequently with clients** – develop a relationship of trust and goodwill, and keep clients informed about any changes which affect them; remember that it is often when there is nothing to report that the client would most appreciate a letter!

6   **Ensure that agreements meet organisational requirements** – consult specialists if you are in doubt.

7   **Optimise agreements** – create a situation whereby you achieve your objectives whilst meeting client needs.

8   **Draw up detailed specifications** – ensure that specifications of the services to be provided contain all the relevant information needed by the client.

9   **Keep accurate records** – include all relevant information about client agreements and implementation plans.

10   **Design client-oriented services** – organise your operations to provide the most efficient service to your clients.

11   **Develop helpful personnel** – encourage all members of your practice to put the clients first and to take personal responsibility for meeting client needs.

■ Planning to meet client needs

1   **Involve relevant people in the planning** – get team members, colleagues, specialists, and even clients themselves, to help you to plan your activities.

2   **Draw on experience** – use information about past successes and failures to prepare your plans.

3   **Plan for contingencies** – make sure your plans can cope with potential changes in circumstances in the future.

4   **Develop realistic plans** – see that they are designed to meet client needs within agreed time-scales and that they identify the resources and skills required to deliver them, with a finance plan and budget.

5   **Develop consistent plans** – see that they are consistent with the practice's key objectives.

6   **Design client-focused services** – organise the practice to provide the most efficient service to the clients.

7   **Discuss your plans** – check that all those involved understand their role in the plans and are committed to making them work.

8   **Promote helpful attitudes** – encourage members of the practice to put clients first and to take personal responsibility for meeting client needs.

■ Meeting client specifications and instructions

1 **Check that specifications and instructions are clear, complete and accurate** – where there is any omission or ambiguity, get clarification from the client. In this respect refer to Section 4.2 'Case management' on page 96 relating to taking instructions in particular cases.

2 **Draw up plans and schedules to meet the specifications and instructions** – allow for contingencies in these plans.

3 **Brief all relevant people** – make sure they understand how the specifications and instructions and the resulting plans and schedules affect them.

4 **Monitor operations** – monitor what is happening and take appropriate action to ensure specifications are met and instructions followed.

5 **Make best use of resources** – use human, capital and financial resources efficiently to meet the requirements.

6 **Encourage all members of the practice to take responsibility for meeting client requirements** – involve everyone in finding the best way to meet specifications and instructions, and gain their commitment.

7 **Give feedback to all members of the practice** – tell them how well they are meeting client requirements.

8 **Get feedback from clients** – use this feedback to improve future activities.

9 **Take corrective action** – implement any changes without delay and inform relevant personnel, colleagues and clients about these.

10 **Monitor corrective action** – make sure that changes are working, and use this experience to improve future operations.

11 **Keep complete and accurate records of activities** – keep records of how well you met client specifications and instructions, and make these records available to appropriate people within the practice.

■ Assuring quality

1   **Be clear about your clients' expectations and requirements** – quality of service means always fulfilling your clients' expectations, and on time.

2   **Consider the relevance of formal quality assurance systems to your practice** – study whether the practice and its clients would benefit from the introduction of a formal quality assurance system of relevance to law practices; consider, in particular, the Law Society's Lexcel certification scheme, the Community Legal Service Quality Mark (CLSQM) of the Legal Services Commission (formerly the Legal Aid Board), Investors in People and ISO 9001: 2000.

3   **Make recommendations for quality assurance systems to meet clients' expectations** – make sure that any systems installed are designed to meet client requirements and not to satisfy a bureaucratic whim.

4   **Encourage all members of the practice to help develop quality assurance systems** – consult those who are most involved with the operation in order to get their ideas and to gain their commitment to following the quality assurance system.

5   **Present details of the quality assurance system, or modifications to it, to all those concerned** – make sure that you brief everyone involved or affected by the quality assurance system about their role or the possible impact on their area.

6   **Encourage people to seek clarification** – check on their understanding of their role and encourage them to ask questions.

7   **Make the best use of resources** – make sure your quality assurance system does not duplicate or add unnecessarily to the workload.

8   **Publicise the benefits and results of quality assurance** – enhance the commitment of the members of the practice and the satisfaction of your clients by making sure that both are aware of the benefits of the quality assurance system.

9   **Monitor your quality assurance systems** – check regularly, at least every year, whether they continue to deliver client satisfaction and make any modifications required.

4.2 Case management

This section is about ensuring that the practice's cases are managed effectively, thereby improving client service and increasing client satisfaction.

The checklists will help you to:

- ensure that matters are properly documented;
- see that risk management procedures are in place;
- ensure compliance with the Solicitors Costs Information and Client Care Code 1999;
- take instructions and terminate matters correctly;
- progress matters and review files;
- handle complaints.

This section is very closely linked to the case management section of the Law Society's Practice Management Standards which are reproduced in full on pages 177 to 190.

The process of 'Case management' looks like this:

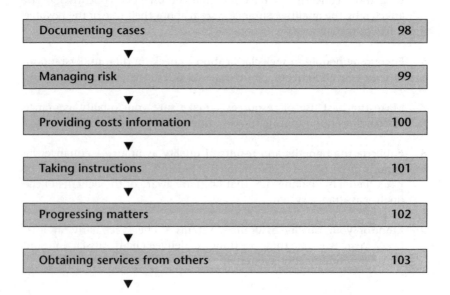

Documenting cases	98
Managing risk	99
Providing costs information	100
Taking instructions	101
Progressing matters	102
Obtaining services from others	103

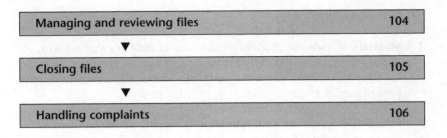

■ Documenting cases

1   **Maintain an index of matters** – maintain an index of matters with all useful information including the name and address and other relevant information concerning the client, the date of the instructions, the type of matter and its source.

2   **Establish a system to facilitate identifying any conflict of interest** – design the index of matters so that it enables conflicts and potential conflicts of interest to be identified at an early stage.

3   **Monitor who is handling matters** – do this in such a way that each fee-earner is only handling matters within his or her capacity.

4   **Maintain a back-up record** – see that all key dates in matters are recorded.

5   **Monitor undertakings** – ensure that all undertakings given on behalf of the practice are properly authorised and subsequently monitored.

6   **Identify multiple matters** – where required to do so by a third party funding the legal costs, or by a client instructing the practice in a number of matters, ensure that there is a system which enables all relevant matters to be identified.

■ Managing risk

1   **Recognise the importance of effective risk management** – to do so should be the policy of the practice in the light of possible claims and the requirements of insurers.

2   **Define responsibility** – see that an overall risk manager for the practice is appointed.

3   **Maintain information** – record the generic risks associated with the types of work carried out by the practice.

4   **List types of case** – list and define the types of case that fall within acceptable risk levels and also those that fall outside acceptable risk levels.

5   **Establish risk procedures** – implement procedures to manage all cases which fall outside acceptable risk levels, including mitigating actions and contingency plans where appropriate.

6   **Review** – conduct an annual documented review of all risk assessment data generated within the practice.

7   **Assess and report risk** – at the beginning of each matter consider whether there is any unusual degree of risk to the practice associated with the matter and record this on the office file. At the end of the case carry out a concluding risk assessment in relation to the case and notify the practice's overall risk manager if the final assessment differs from the initial assessment, and provide a written explanation.

■ Providing costs information

1   **Establish a written procedure** – this is necessary to ensure compliance with the Solicitors Costs Information and Client Care Code 1999 and to provide for clear and regular communication with clients, third parties and the court as necessary in relation to costs.

2   **Reveal the basis of charging** – provide the client with advance costs information.

3   **Estimate likely cost** – give the best information possible about likely cost, including a breakdown between fees, VAT and disbursements.

4   **Explain time** – where time spent is a factor in the calculation of fees provide a clear explanation of the time likely to be spent on the matter.

5   **Provide a range of costs** – when agreeing a fixed fee, giving a realistic estimate or giving a forecast, provide a range of costs.

6   **Inform about possible changes** – tell the client if any estimate is not intended to be fixed and if charging rates may be increased.

7   **Consider upper limits** – explain to a private paying client that the client may set an upper limit on the practice's costs, which may be reached without further authority.

8   **Explain foreseeable payments** – explain to the client the reasonably foreseeable payments which may be required to be paid to the practice or to a third party, and when these payments may be needed.

9   **Update** – make arrangements for updating costs information and inform the client at regular intervals of at least every six months.

10 **Explain public funding** – if the client may be eligible for public funding, explain the costs implications for the client, particularly in relation to the statutory charge, where applicable.

11 **Explain insurance issues** – if the client's liability for costs may be covered by insurance or another party, such as a trade union, or if the client's liability for another party's costs may be so covered, inform the client accordingly.

■ Taking instructions

1   **Establish a documented procedure** – this will help ensure that cases are handled in a consistent way.

2   **Have regard to non-discrimination** – in accepting instructions from clients and in the provision of services, respect the guidance issued by the Law Society from time to time.

3   **Agree and record** – document the client's instructions and objectives, a clear explanation of the issues raised and the advice given, the action to be taken by the practice and the likely time-scale, the strategy decided upon and any case plan.

4   **Name the responsible person** – record the name and status of the person dealing with the matter and the name of the person responsible for its overall supervision.

5   **Nominate a contact in the event of a problem** – record the name of the person to contact about any problem with the service provided.

6   **Confirm to the client** – confirm all these matters with the client (ordinarily in writing) and provide written information to the client about complaints procedures.

7   **Identify key dates** – identify key dates in the matter and record these in the file and in the back-up system.

8   **Discuss expense and risk** – discuss with the client whether the likely outcome will justify the expense or risk involved, including, if relevant, the risk of having to bear an opponent's costs.

9   **Consider risk to the practice** – consider whether there is any unusual degree of risk to the practice associated with the matter, record this on the office file and inform the practice's risk manager.

■ Progressing matters

1   **Establish a documented procedure** – this will help ensure that cases are handled in a consistent way.

2   **Inform on progress** – give the client, at appropriate intervals, information on the progress of the matter (or reasons for the lack of progress).

3   **Inform about changes** – give the client promptly information about changes in the action planned to be taken in the matter, strategy or case plan, its handling (including the person with conduct) or cost.

4   **Inform about risk** – tell the client in writing of any circumstances which will or may affect the degree of risk involved or cost benefit to the client of continuing with the matter.

5   **Respond** – respond in a timely manner to correspondence and telephone calls.

6   **Provide cost information** – give to the client in writing at least every six months information on cost and, in publicly funded cases, the effect of the statutory charge if any, and make timely reference to the client when an agreed limit on costs or stage in the process is approached.

7   **Give speedy information about adverse costs orders** – in litigation matters tell the client immediately about adverse costs orders as payment may be required forthwith.

8   **Consider a case plan** – in a complex matter consider preparing a case plan, agreeing it with the client and periodically reviewing and updating it.

■ Obtaining services from others

1   **Establish a written procedure** – this will help ensure that all those called upon to provide external services are handled in a consistent way.

2   **Define the providers of services carefully** – services may be provided by barristers, expert witnesses and others.

3   **Use clear selection criteria** – these should not discriminate in relation to gender, sexual orientation, race, disability or religion.

4   **Consult with the client** – where appropriate, consult with the client in relation to selection of service providers and give proper advice to the client on the choice of advocate.

5   **Maintain records** – keep a record (centrally, by department, or by office) on barristers, experts and other service providers used.

6   **Give clear instructions** – describe clearly what is required of the service provider and see that the instructions, in litigation matters, comply with the rules of court and any court orders.

7   **Check the opinions and reports received** – ensure that they provide adequate information (and, in litigation matters, comply with the rules of court and any court orders).

8   **Pay fees** – see that there is a procedure that ensures payment of the fees of service providers.

■ Managing and reviewing files

1 **Establish a documented procedure** – this will help ensure that cases are handled in a consistent way.

2 **Facilitate checking** – ensure that the status of a matter can be easily checked by other members of the practice.

3 **Arrange documents** – see that documents are arranged in the file in an orderly way.

4 **Show key information** – see that key information is shown clearly on the file (for example at the front of the file) which will include undertakings given on behalf of the practice.

5 **See that a supervisor is available** – a suitably qualified person should be available for each matter to provide guidance and assistance in the event of need.

6 **Allocate work** – work should be allocated in relation to the qualifications and experience of fee-earners and their workloads.

7 **Review case files** – there should be arrangements for the management of case files to be reviewed periodically and the review should be carried out by a fee-earner who has not been involved in the day-to-day conduct of the matter.

8 **Record the review** – a record of the review should be kept on the case file and on a central record.

9 **Carry out corrective action** – there should be arrangements to ensure that any corrective action resulting from the review is carried out promptly.

10 **Consider the frequency of reviews** – consideration should be given as to the frequency of case reviews and whether all files are reviewed or a sample selected.

11 **Consider other and further arrangements** – practices may also adopt other arrangements to ensure the appropriate supervision of casework and options include checking the incoming post, the signature of outgoing post by a supervisor and regular review sessions with a supervisor. These latter may cover new cases taken on and the discussion of case plans in complex cases, progress reviews for current cases, the evaluation of completed cases and consideration of training needs in relation to legal knowledge and skills.

■ Closing files

1 **Establish a documented procedure** – this will help ensure that cases are handled in a consistent way.

2 **Report the outcome** – report to the client on the outcome and explain any further action that the client is required to take in the matter and what (if anything) the practice will do.

3 **Account to the client** – account for any outstanding money.

4 **Return property** – return to the client original documents and other property belonging to the client if required (save for items which are by agreement to be stored by the practice).

5 **Advise about arrangements for storage** – advise the client about arrangements for storage and retrieval of papers and other items retained but check first that this has not been dealt with already, for example, in terms of business.

6 **Advise about future reviews** – advise clients whether they should review the matter in the future and, if so, when.

7 **Assess risk** – carry out a concluding risk assessment in relation to the case and notify the practice's overall risk manager if the final assessment differs from the initial assessment, providing a written explanation.

■ Handling complaints

1 **Establish documented arrangements** – this will help ensure that all complaints are handled in a consistent way.

2 **Take a positive attitude to complaint procedures** – remember that, because the Office for the Supervision of Solicitors suggests that a satisfied client may tell five people on average of their experience whereas a dissatisfied client may tell 23 people on average, it is important to deal efficiently with complaints, particularly given that referral and recommendation remain your most important sources of new work.

3 **Define the complaint** – see that the complaint is recorded in writing immediately, even if it is expressed orally.

4 **Make the procedure accessible** – see that all clients are provided with a copy of the complaints procedure on request.

5 **Report and record** – report and record centrally every complaint made by a client.

6 **Respond** – respond appropriately to any complaint within a defined timetable.

7 **Identify the cause** – identify the cause of any problem of which a client has complained, offering any appropriate redress, and correcting any unsatisfactory procedures.

8 **Review** – perform an annual documented review of any complaints to establish issues where the client care may be improved, including clients' perceptions of the procedure itself.

9 **Appoint a client complaints partner** – see that a senior partner or the managing partner is made responsible for all aspects of the complaints procedure.

10 **Avoid appearing defensive** – on receipt of a complaint try to resolve problems or misunderstandings immediately. Do not forget that saying 'sorry' does not mean that you are necessarily admitting fault or liability, and that this will generally be all the client requires. Do not become defensive and do not try to avoid the client as this will almost certainly make matters worse.

11 **Keep the client informed** – tell the client how you plan to resolve the problem, how long it will take and give the client progress reports where appropriate.

12 **Implement the solution promptly** – once the solution has been identified, take prompt action to solve the client's problem and inform the client of the action taken.

13 **Monitor the delivery of the solution** – and make appropriate modifications to resolve any problems that may arise again.

5

Managing the practice

Managing the practice involves:

5.1   Organising the practice

This section is about ensuring that the practice is organised effectively in order to provide excellent client service.

The checklists will help you to:

- obtain the financial resources you require to set up or expand the practice;
- establish an appropriate management structure for the practice;
- develop operating plans to achieve your objectives;
- develop a marketing plan and evaluate marketing activities;
- administer the office(s).

The process of 'Organising the practice' looks like this:

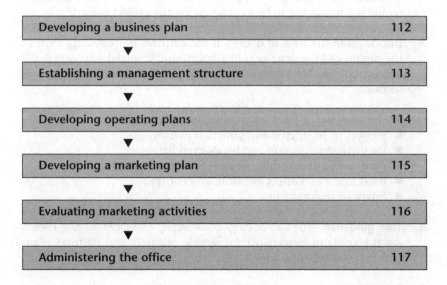

Developing a business plan	112

▼

Establishing a management structure	113

▼

Developing operating plans	114

▼

Developing a marketing plan	115

▼

Evaluating marketing activities	116

▼

Administering the office	117

■ Developing a business plan

1   **Be clear about the purpose of a business plan** – on setting up a practice or setting up a new venture for the practice you will almost certainly need to produce a business plan; this will need to show what you intend to do and to demonstrate to potential financial backers, including almost certainly to your bank, how you are going to finance the operation.

2   **Use professional financial help** – the majority of people setting up a new business will go to an accountant to prepare the business plan and there is no reason at all why solicitors should act differently.

3   **Do research** – you must research into potential market sectors, profit levels, setting up costs, etc. and you will need accountancy assistance to present these in financial terms.

4   **Calculate the costings** – you will need to show what the capital requirement is going to be in order to get the project underway.

5   **Decide upon the level of detail** – if the partners are providing most of the capital and the practice is in a flourishing financial state, less detail will be required but business plans will almost always contain certain sections:

   ■ summary of the proposed project, including the business objectives;
   ■ services to be offered and potential market;
   ■ fee income projection and break-even figure;
   ■ profit and loss account and cash flow forecasts;
   ■ fixed assets and assets available as security;
   ■ financial requirements.

6   **Take guidance** – the Law Society book *Setting Up and Managing a Small Practice* contains precedents for simple business and costings plans which you might find useful.

7   **Base the plan on any existing marketing plan** – if the business plan is needed to obtain further finance for an existing practice use any existing marketing plan as its basis.

■ Establishing a management structure

1   **Review possible types of management structure** – there are many different types of structure appropriate to legal practices and these can vary from setting up a management board, naming a managing partner or appointing a non-lawyer chief executive. Solicitors may also practise in corporate form, subject to compliance with the Solicitors' Incorporated Practice Rules 1988.

2   **Ensure that the management structure meets the needs of the practice** – see that the management structure is appropriate for the partners, principals and staff, the location of the practice and the type of work it does.

3   **Name the persons who are in charge** – see that:

   ■ there is a named supervisor for each area of legal work (a supervisor may be responsible for more than one area);
   ■ the supervisor has appropriate experience of the work supervised, to be able to guide and assist others;
   ■ supervisors are able to describe their experience and the ways in which they guide and assist those under their supervision.

4   **List the responsibilities** – list the designated responsibilities of individuals in the practice (including responsibility for adherence to any relevant management standards).

5   **Name committees, if any, and establish their terms of reference** – see that the terms of reference of any committees are appropriately summarised and documented.

6   **Establish reporting structures** – see that there are clearly documented reporting structures within the practice and describe the reporting structures, for example, in the form of a 'family tree'.

7   **Produce a written description** – produce a written description of the practice's management structure and distribute is to, for example, incoming partners, principals and staff.

■ Developing operating plans

1   **Define the real need** – operating plans can be used in many circum-stances to match the resources and skills available to the tasks to be performed.

2   **Ensure consistency** – see that all operating plans are based upon the mission and key objectives of the practice.

3   **Develop only those plans that are needed** – apart from a marketing plan, many practices will not need more than a finance plan and budget together with an information technology strategy, so long as the mission and key objectives of the practice have been defined and developed.

4   **Consult widely** – obtain input from all interested parties as this will ensure commitment.

5   **Measure results** – compare the relevant plan with current performance on a regular basis, at least quarterly.

6   **Retain flexibility** – remember that nothing goes exactly as expected, so be prepared to amend plans to cope with unexpected developments.

7   **Avoid excess paper** – keep all plans short: because of the information explosion, most people are drowned in paper and remember that, as a result, few read more than the first page of a document with attention.

■ Developing a marketing plan

1   **Ensure consistency with the mission and key objectives of the practice** – see that the marketing plan is derived from the practice's mission statement and is consistent with the practice's key objectives.

2   **Review the current quality and level of activity** – if this is satisfactory, a marketing plan will need to be less detailed than for a practice wishing to expand, develop a new speciality, or which is uncertain about its future client base.

3   **Decide whether or not the current situation is satisfactory** – for some areas of work, the marketing plan may need to describe how to contain demand to an acceptable level rather than how to encourage more work of a defined type, taking into account that work's profitability and the limited resources of the practice.

4   **Ensure the contents of the plan are complete** – describe:

   - the services to be provided and the client groups to be served;
   - how the services will be delivered and the practice's client care policy in this regard;
   - the practice's resources, including skills and knowledge;
   - the objectives for the clients or the activity to be developed;
   - how the practice will be developed to attain the objectives.

5   **Concentrate particularly on developing the existing client base** – much more work will come from repeat business from satisfied clients and from their recommendations to others than from other sources.

6   **Consider your communications options** – decide upon the best communications mix of public relations and practice promotion, even advertising if appropriate, taking into account the potential client audience, the relative benefit and cost, and the compatibility with the values and key objectives of your practice.

7   **Set up a method to implement the plan** – provide a timetable and a budget and allocate and describe individual responsibilities for the marketing activities, with consequent variation of existing chargeable time objectives.

8   **Monitor the response** – ensure that there are arrangements for monitoring the results of the marketing effort; see, in particular, that there are records of the sources of referrals.

■ Evaluating marketing activities

1   **Monitor activities against plans** – check regularly to ensure that marketing activities are being undertaken according to plan.

2   **Monitor performance against budgets** – check regularly to ensure that marketing activities are delivering the expected results.

3   **Clarify ambiguous information** – where information for monitoring is lacking or is unclear, take action promptly to obtain valid information.

4   **Provide information to authorised people** – let authorised people have the monitoring information promptly, but ensure that the required level of confidentiality is maintained.

5   **Evaluate marketing performance against key objectives** – check whether the key objectives defined in your strategic plan are being met.

6   **Consult about variances** – where there are significant variances in performance against plan, consult with appropriate colleagues and decide upon the best course of action to correct the situation and to minimise any adverse effects.

7   **Take action in case of variances** – take prompt corrective action where performance is significantly different from that expected.

8   **Inform people of the implications of variances** – let relevant people know promptly of the financial effects of variances.

9   **Communicate any changes of plan** – make sure that all those involved or affected are aware of the changes and their revised responsibilities.

■ Administering the office

1   **Designate and document administrative responsibilities** – see that, as part of the practice's management structure, administrative responsibilities are designated, including the facilities needed to provide services, together with those relating to maintenance and support, health and safety conditions and an annual review of risk. See that the issues addressed in the review of risk include health and safety considerations.

2   **Establish and maintain an office manual** – collate information on office practice in the form of an office manual available to all members of the practice. In particular, see that there are documented procedures to note each page with the date and/or number of issue, to review the manual at least annually and to record the dates of amendments. Note that a template for an office manual, which includes precedents for forms and procedures, is available in the *Lexcel Office Procedures Manual*.

3   **Establish a document and filing system** – provide a system to ensure that the practice is able to trace all documents, correspondence and other information and that these are properly stored and readily accessible.

4   **Make arrangements for proper file management** – in order to assist in the management of individual cases, see that there is a procedure to ensure that:

   ■ the status of matters can be easily checked;
   ■ documents are arranged in an orderly way;
   ■ key information is shown clearly, including details of any undertakings given on behalf of the practice.

5   **Provide access to legal reference material** – set up a system so that lawyers have ready access to up-to-date legal reference material for the areas in which the practice offers a service and see that lawyers receive timely information about changes in the law, practice and procedure relevant to their work.

5.2 Managing change

This section is about identifying, implementing and evaluating improvements.

The checklists will help you to:

- look for areas of the practice where improvements can be made;
- assess the benefits and disadvantages arising from the changes;
- prepare plans to make improvement;
- consult all concerned to get them to agree to the changes;
- implement plans for change;
- evaluate whether improvements have been achieved.

The process of 'Managing change' looks like this:

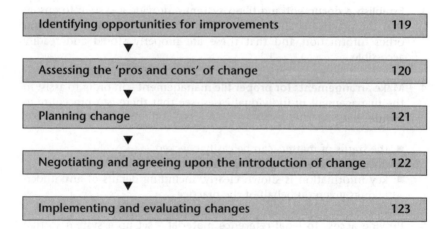

Identifying opportunities for improvements	119
Assessing the 'pros and cons' of change	120
Planning change	121
Negotiating and agreeing upon the introduction of change	122
Implementing and evaluating changes	123

■ Identifying opportunities for improvements

1   **Keep up to date with developments** – make sure you get relevant, valid, reliable information from various sources on all developments, not only in law and practice, but also in equipment and technology.

2   **Consider the importance of these developments to the practice** – carry out a regular review of developments and analyse their significance to the practice.

3   **Pass on information about developments to the appropriate people** – if you think they are important, make sure your colleagues and all other members of the practice are aware of their significance.

4   **Identify opportunities for improvements** – use information on developments to identify opportunities for growth, improvements in procedures or improvements in quality.

5   **Monitor and evaluate your methods of practice continuously** – always look for areas where improvements could be made and take appropriate action.

6   **Identify any obstacles to change** – take appropriate measures to alleviate any problems which may prevent improvements being made.

7   **Learn from your experience** – use your experience of previous improvements to help identify new ones.

■ Assessing the 'pros and cons' of change

1   **Get as complete and accurate information as possible** – make sure you have sufficient information on both current and proposed services and methods to allow you to make a reliable assessment.

2   **Compare the advantages and disadvantages** – use qualitative and quantitative techniques to assess the 'pros and cons' of current and proposed services and methods.

3   **Assess the implications of introducing changes** – changes may affect cash flow, working practices, personnel morale and client loyalty, therefore anticipate and assess the likely effect of changes.

4   **Take into account previous assessments of changes** – look at whether previous assessments turned out to be realistic and modify your current assessment accordingly.

5   **Present your recommendations to the appropriate people** – make your recommendations to your senior colleagues and to others involved, in a way which helps them take a decision and allows time for the decision to be put into effect.

6   **Amend your recommendations in the light of responses** – make appropriate alterations to your recommendations on the basis of the responses you get from your senior colleagues and others.

■ Planning change

1   **Provide clear and accurate information** – let those affected know about the proposed change in time for them to prepare effectively.

2   **Get people involved** – give people the chance to comment on the proposed change and to help in the planning of the implementation.

3   **Make the case for change** – give a clear and convincing rationale for the change and support this with sound evidence.

4   **Identify potential obstacles to change** – and when you have done so find effective ways of avoiding or overcoming these obstacles.

5   **Develop a detailed plan** – see that it includes:

- the rationale;
- the aim and objectives of the change;
- how it will be implemented;
- who will be involved and their individual roles;
- the resources required;
- the time-scale;
- how the plan will be monitored;
- how you will know that the change has been successful.

■ Negotiating and agreeing upon the introduction of change

1   **Present information on projected change to the appropriate people –** let colleagues and other members of the practice know about the change at the earliest possible time, and in sufficient detail, to allow them to evaluate its impact on their area of responsibility.

2   **Conduct negotiations in a spirit of goodwill –** make sure you retain the support of others and find mutually acceptable ways of settling any disputes.

3   **Make compromises where appropriate –** it may be necessary to make compromises to accommodate other priorities, but make sure these are consistent with the practice's mission and key objectives.

4   **Reach an agreement in line with the practice's strategy –** and include detailed implementation plans.

5   **Keep records of negotiations and agreements –** make sure your records are complete and accurate and that they are available for others to refer to if necessary.

6   **Where you could not secure the changes you planned, tell the members of your team in a positive manner –** sometimes you are disappointed at not being able to obtain the changes you wanted for your team, due to other organisational priorities; explain the reasons for this in a positive way.

7   **Encourage all relevant people to understand and participate in the changes –** communicate the changes and their effects to people, and gain their support.

■ Implementing and evaluating changes

1 **Present details of implementation plans to all concerned** – make sure that everyone involved or affected is briefed about the changes and the possible impact upon them.

2 **Encourage people to seek clarification** – check on their understanding of their role and encourage them to ask questions.

3 **Use resources in the most effective way** – plan carefully so that you meet the new requirements as cost-effectively as possible.

4 **Monitor the changes** – check to see that the changes have been implemented according to plan and that they result in the improvements anticipated.

5 **Evaluate the benefits of the changes** – compare the new way of working with the old: are the benefits as expected?

6 **Modify implementation plans and activities in the light of experience** – you may need to modify the way you implement changes to cope with unforeseen problems.

7 **Review the change process** – review the whole process of identifying, assessing, negotiating, agreeing, implementing and evaluating change; note ways of doing it better next time and make appropriate recommendations to senior colleagues and specialists.

5.3 Project management

There are many projects to be managed within a practice and they can be very varied: from establishing a new speciality to setting up a new knowledge management infrastructure. Sometimes a client may request that the practice undertake a project, for example, take over the services previously provided by an internal legal department. This section is about managing projects on time, within budget and to the standard of quality required.

The checklists will help you to:

- arrive at a shared understanding of the goals and scope of the project;
- develop a detailed plan to deliver the project outcomes on time;
- estimate the costs involved and develop and agree a realistic budget;
- monitor the project and take action in the event of contingencies or significant deviations from plan;
- deliver the project effectively, provide feedback to those involved and develop opportunities for new work.

As a project manager, you will find that many of the other checklists in the operational management area (managing change, people, finance, resources and information, for example) will be of use to you during the course of a project.

The process of 'Project management' looks like this:

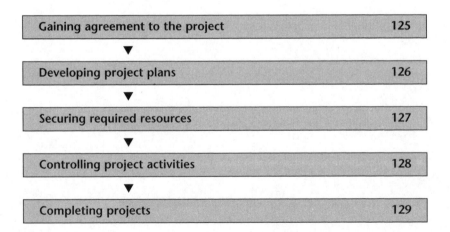

Gaining agreement to the project	125
Developing project plans	126
Securing required resources	127
Controlling project activities	128
Completing projects	129

■ Gaining agreement to the project

1   **Clarify and agree upon the project goals with your client** – whether your client is within the practice or from outside, discuss and settle what is expected as a result of the project.

2   **Identify the constraints on the project** – constraints may be internal to the project (e.g. do you have the necessary resources and technology?), internal to the practice (e.g. are the financial objectives achievable, does the project fit with the key objectives of the practice?) or external (e.g. logistical, regulatory or environmental issues).

3   **Check that the project is viable** – are the goals realistic within the time and resources allowed for the project?

4   **Agree upon the quality and success criteria** – define the specific quality to which the project must be delivered, and agree how successful completion will be measured.

5   **Identify and assess risks to the project** – consider

- the things that may go wrong with the project;
- how likely they are to go wrong;
- what you can do to minimise the risk or the effects of things going wrong;
- what contingency plans you can make.

6   **Settle the outline management structure for the project** – how is the work going to be broken down, who will be responsible for what and what reports will be made with what frequency?

7   **Agree upon the terms of the project contract** – if your client is external to the practice, draw up and sign an agreement which covers all the key points relating to the project; if your client is internal, draw up a memorandum of understanding in similar form.

8   **Review the scope of the project** – periodically check to make sure that the project's goal and scope are fundamentally the same and, if they have changed substantially, renegotiate your agreement or memorandum of understanding.

■ Developing project plans

1   **Clarify the scope of the project with all concerned** – make sure that everyone involved understands the scope and goals of the project and their roles within it.

2   **Break the work down into manageable packages** – divide up a major project into mini-projects or work packages which have defined objectives.

3   **Define the schedule of work packages** – decide which activities have to be completed before other activities can start (those on the 'critical path') and those that can take place at the same time; make sure that all activities can be completed before the end date of the project.

4   **Allocate responsibilities for work packages** – settle with those managing work packages (whether they work inside or outside the practice) exactly for what they are responsible, what you expect to be delivered, when, and for what cost.

5   **Agree upon working methods** – settle with those responsible the methods they will use to deliver the work and the level of autonomy they have for changing working methods.

6   **Agree upon reporting and monitoring procedures** – settle with the internal or external client and with the work-package managers

   - how progress will be reported;
   - delivery dates for work packages;
   - at what point significant deviations from the plan must be reported.

7   **Define communication procedures** – settle the procedures for regular communication on project progress and for communication in the event of emergencies or contingencies.

■ Securing required resources

1   **Estimate the costs of the project** – look at the resources required for each work package, including

- labour costs;
- materials costs;
- equipment costs;
- transport costs;
- general costs;
- overhead costs.

2   **Estimate the human resources required** – look at the number and type of people required and the different skills they will need.

3   **Estimate the physical resources required** – look at the equipment, materials, premises, services and transport you will need.

4   **Estimate the overhead cost** – what is the proportion of costs of management time, office costs and consumables which you should allocate to the project?

5   **Take account of contingencies** – make allowance for the things that may go wrong.

6   **Allow for inflation** – if the project is to run over a year or more make sure that you allow for any likely increases in costs.

7   **Settle your project budget** – present your overall budget to your internal or external client, agree upon this budget and how payments and reimbursements will be made.

■ Controlling project activities

1   **Agree upon a baseline plan with all concerned** – make sure that every-one involved – the internal or external client, the work package managers and those working on the project – agree to working to, and reporting against, your baseline project plan.

2   **Authorise any changes** – make sure that you (and your internal or external client, where appropriate) are informed of, and agree to, any significant changes to project activities or working practices.

3   **Get regular and accurate progress reports** – make sure that you receive progress reports on time, and that these report progress against plan accurately.

4   **Evaluate your progress** – evaluate whether progress is satisfactory and forecast whether the project's objectives will be delivered on time and within budget.

5   **Discuss your progress** – discuss the progress of the project with your internal or external client, work package managers and those working on the project to confirm the actual situation.

6   **Take corrective action if required** – if necessary, take appropriate action to get the project back on track to deliver the project's objectives.

7   **Respond effectively to contingencies** – take appropriate action in the event of emergencies and contingencies and report the situation to your internal or external client as soon as possible.

8   **Settle changes to the scope of the project** – if the scope of the project, its objectives or the client's requirements have changed, agree these changes and their implications with the client, whether internal or external.

9   **Revise the project plan** – make sure that all those involved are aware of the changes and how they affect them.

■ Completing projects

1   **Deliver the results of the project** – hand over the product of the project to your internal or external client.

2   **Confirm the success of the project** – confirm to the client that the goals and objectives have been achieved to the quality required and against agreed success criteria and obtain the client's agreement to this.

3   **Evaluate your project** – consider what went well and what went badly and identify and evaluate the reasons for the success and failure and the lessons to be learned.

4   **Provide feedback to those involved** – provide feedback on performance to work package managers, others working on the project and also to your internal or external client on how they contributed to the success of the project.

5   **Celebrate the completion of the project** – take appropriate opportunities to celebrate your shared success and thank and congratulate those involved.

6   **Publicise your achievements** – look for opportunities to let others know of the success of the project and your organisation's role in it.

7   **Develop follow-up opportunities** – make the most of the opportunity to identify and develop potential new projects with the client, whether internal or external, and with others having an interest in the success of the project.

6

Managing finance

Managing finance is about organising the availability of the financial information necessary to run the practice, establishing and agreeing upon budgets and ensuring that there is sufficient cash to run the practice profitably.

It involves:

6.1   Financial organisation

This section is about making sure that there is a system which will provide enough financial information for the effective management of the practice.

The checklists will help you to:

- monitor income and expenditure;
- secure the information necessary to run the practice;
- get the best from information technology.

The process for 'Financial organisation' looks like this:

Financial and management information	134

▼

Computerisation and time-recording	135

■ Financial and management information

1   **Allocate and document responsibility** – the practice may have to demonstrate to providers of finance or to major clients that there is a specific person within the practice who exercises responsibility for financial affairs.

2   **Set up a financial information system** – the practice needs to have sufficient information to monitor income, expenditure and cost and to allow forward planning and the system must provide this information on a reliable basis.

3   **Ensure that the financial system provides information on profitability of work** – it is not enough to have an unfounded belief that all work is profitable; the accurate measurement of profitability is essential.

4   **Link the system to the accounts** – practices need to produce:

   ■ an annual budget, including any proposed capital expenditure;
   ■ an analysis of income and expenditure against budget, on a quarterly basis;
   ■ an annual profit and loss account;
   ■ an annual balance sheet;
   ■ an annual cash flow forecast; and
   ■ a quarterly variance analysis of cash flow.

5   **Decide about disclosure** – practices will not normally disclose financial information to third parties; but, for example, they may in appropriate cases instead make available an accountant's certificate that systems to provide the relevant information within the practice itself are in place.

6   **Keep management sufficiently informed** – the practice may find it helpful to maintain more complete management information by, for example, providing:

   ■ a separate capital expenditure budget;
   ■ weekly or monthly aged lists of debtors;
   ■ analyses of:
      – the cost of services,
      – cases, by category and client name,
      – fees by fee-earner, category or department,
      – working capital.

■ Computerisation and time-recording

1 **Implement a computerised accounting system** – this will assist cost-effectiveness and it is unlikely that the practice could comply with management standards in the absence of computerisation; simplify all manual record systems before mechanising them; ensure that the system is consistent with the information technology strategy of the practice.

2 **Take advice before implementation** – contact appropriate consultants for relevant information.

3 **Plan carefully** – there is a significant cost in money and time attached to planning for development of information technology, including the purchase of software and training and support following implementation but, if properly planned, this investment is worthwhile.

4 **Provide back-up and parallel systems** – computer systems do not always work as expected first time, so consider retaining manual and other systems until you are satisfied with the new installation.

5 **Check that your time-recording system is still appropriate for your current needs** – it is necessary for all firms to have a documented system that ensures that time spent on casework is properly recorded and attributed and many systems introduced some time ago need updating.

6 **Choose an appropriate system** – computerised accounting systems can maintain financial records as required by the Solicitors' Accounts Rules 1998 and provide other reports information as well; details of these systems are given in *Software Solutions: a Guide to Legal Software* (Law Society).

7 **Follow guidance** – consult Section 8.1 'Introducing information technology' on page 155 before implementation of any computerised accounting and time-recording system.

6.2 Managing budgets

This section is about making sure that the financial targets of the practice are met.

The checklists will help you to:

- prepare estimates of fee income and of expenditure;
- negotiate effectively with those who have to approve the budget;
- compare actual expenditure with the budget on a regular basis and make any appropriate modifications.

The process for 'Managing budgets' looks like this:

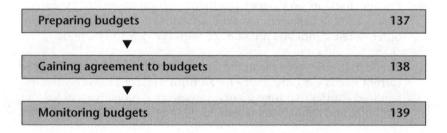

Preparing budgets	137

▼

Gaining agreement to budgets	138

▼

Monitoring budgets	139

■ Preparing budgets

1   **Prepare accurate estimates of benefits, income and costs** – base your estimates on valid, reliable information; include historical data and information about trends where it is available.

2   **Assess alternative courses of action** – before submitting your budget and recommending expenditure, assess the relative benefits and costs of alternative courses of action.

3   **Encourage all relevant members of the practice to contribute** – if people are involved in the process of drawing up the budget, they will be more committed to achieving the desired results and to keeping within agreed financial limits.

4   **Indicate the benefits clearly** – be sure to specify the net benefit which will be gained, over time, from the expenditure.

5   **State your assumptions** – make it clear what assumptions you have made and why.

6   **Allow for contingencies** – take into account any future changes which may affect the level of fee and other income and expenditure.

7   **Check your budgets with others** – where other people have been involved in providing information or making suggestions, check the details with them before submitting a final budget.

8   **Present your budget clearly and concisely** – make use of any forms which the practice may have developed for presenting budgets.

9   **Be prepared to give a fuller explanation** – have all your information and arguments to hand to counter challenges to your proposed budget.

10   **Learn from your experience** – compare actual costs and benefits with the budget and use this information to help you to improve the preparation of a budget in the future

■ Gaining agreement to budgets

1 **Prepare people in advance** – involve colleagues and your team, and those who will be approving the budgets, in discussing assumptions and drawing up the budget.

2 **State your assumptions and the contingencies allowed for** – make it clear what assumptions you have made and what contingencies you have allowed for.

3 **Present your budget clearly and concisely** – make use of any forms the practice may have developed for presenting budgets and emphasise the benefits to the practice.

4 **Be as accurate as you can in your estimates** – use all the information available to support your calculations.

5 **Allow sufficient time for negotiation** – present your budget sufficiently early to allow you to provide further information if required.

6 **Negotiate with a spirit of goodwill** – show that you intend to find a mutually acceptable solution.

7 **Seek clarification, where there is uncertainty or disagreement** – ask relevant people for guidance and help in finding an acceptable solution.

8 **Publish the budget decisions** – tell all those with an interest in the outcome of budget negotiation about the decisions taken promptly, in order to secure their support, co-operation and confidence.

■ Monitoring budgets

1   **Get people involved** – encourage members of the practice and of your team to take individual and collective responsibility to control activities against budgets.

2   **Check actual income and expenditure against budgets** – get accurate information on fee income and costs at appropriate intervals.

3   **Keep expenditure within agreed limits** – be clear about your budget limits and make sure you keep within them; check that all expenditure conforms to the practice's policies and procedures.

4   **Phase expenditure according to a planned timescale** – make sure you do not overspend your budget in any period, as this will be detrimental to cash flow, even if you are still within budget for the year.

5   **Report any likely over- or under-spend against budget** – let the appropriate people know as soon as possible of any potential variation against budget.

6   **Report any likely variation in fee income against budget** – let the appropriate people know as soon as possible if fee and other income is likely to be under or over budget.

7   **Give the reasons for any variations** – analyse the causes for variations in income or expenditure and propose corrective action.

8   **Take prompt corrective action** – take appropriate action where there are actual or potential significant deviations from budget.

9   **Get authority for changes in allocations between budgets** – where you need to spend more from one budget and less from another, obtain any necessary authorisation.

10 **Get approval for changes to budgets** – where you need to change your budget during the accounting period, get approval from the appropriate authority.

6.3   Controlling finances

This section is about ensuring the financial viability of the practice through disciplined cost control, billing and fee recovery, the management of cash flow and credit control.

The checklists will help you to:

- reduce the practice's need for external financial support;
- keep a tight control over expenditure;
- ensure that there is sufficient cash to fund the activities of the practice;
- reduce bad debts to a minimum; and
- increase the profits of the practice.

The process of 'Controlling finances' looks like this:

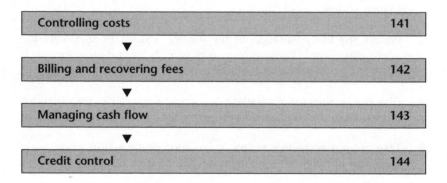

Controlling costs	141
Billing and recovering fees	142
Managing cash flow	143
Credit control	144

■ Controlling costs

1 **Make every member of the practice and of your team aware of how they can help to control costs** – get them to consider areas where costs could be reduced and bring to their attention costs they could help to reduce.

2 **Keep expenditure within agreed budgets** – know what the budget limits are and check that you keep within them.

3 **Where expenditure is outside your responsibility, refer requests promptly to the appropriate authority** – many costs are the responsibility of another part of the practice; let the appropriate people know promptly if you need their authorisation for expenditure.

4 **Keep records of expenditure** – keep accurate and complete records available for reference.

5 **Assess information on costs and the use of resources carefully** – regular reviews of costs will help you identify areas where these can be reduced or where there can be a better use of resources.

6 **Look for improvements** – make recommendations for improvements in efficiency as quickly as possible to the appropriate people.

7 **Take prompt corrective action** – where expenditure is likely to exceed budget, report this immediately to the appropriate authority and take action to minimise the effects.

■ Billing and recovering fees

1   **See that clients are informed of billing practices** – at the outset of a matter, ensure that you reach an agreement with the client on the method of billing and, if possible, the eventual amount of the bill; to achieve this follow the 'Providing costs information' checklist contained in Section 4.2 'Case management' on p. 100.

2   **Obtain payments on account of costs** – you may, at the outset of a retainer, require the client to make a payment on account of costs and disbursements to be incurred.

3   **Send bills on time** – render a bill of costs within a reasonable time of concluding the matter to which the bill relates.

4   **Provide sufficient information** – your bill of costs must provide sufficient information to identify the matter to which it relates, and the period covered.

5   **Keep a record of unpaid accounts** – it may seem obvious, but always know how much money your clients owe and how long the accounts have been outstanding.

6   **Recover moneys owing** – do not hesitate to take action to recover monies owed: in particular, do not write off unpaid bills automatically, and consider the relevant VAT and other tax considerations involved in writing off bills.

■ Managing cash flow

1   **Prepare a cash flow forecast** – get full information on expected receipts and payments to determine the likely pattern of cash flows over the accounting period.

2   **Consider all the factors** – these may include regular receipts and payments, capital payments, partners' drawings, disbursements, and exceptional receipts and payments.

3   **Prepare cash budgets** – present your budgets in the approved format, clearly indicating the net cash required for each period.

4   **Monitor receipts and payments** – monitor cash receipts and payments against budgeted cash flow.

5   **Take prompt corrective action** – in the event of significant actual or potential deviations from the cash budget, take appropriate action such as arranging overdraft facilities, investing surplus cash or expediting debt collection.

6   **Manage the cash balances** – anticipate surpluses and deficits and take appropriate action, taking into account trends in the financial or economic environment.

7   **Invest surplus funds** – invest any surplus funds in marketable securities, following carefully any financial procedures and authorisation limits the practice may have.

8   **Arrange overdraft or loan facilities where required** – anticipate the need to for an overdraft or loan so as to get the most favourable terms possible.

9   **Maintain an adequate level of liquidity** – keep sufficient cash readily available to meet known requirements and possible contingencies.

10 **Maintain the security of cash** – always observe the practice's financial regulations and security procedures when handling cash.

■ Credit control

1   **Establish and comply with the practice's credit policy** – whenever you settle credit terms with a client ensure that you comply with the practice's policy in this regard.

2   **Run credit checks** – use valid information sources to ensure that current and potential clients are credit-worthy and only take new instructions from clients who are credit-worthy.

3   **Present bills promptly** – send bills to clients on the agreed date, clearly specifying any credit terms agreed.

4   **Monitor your debtors' accounts regularly** – analyse key indicators such as the age analysis of debtors, the average periods of any credit given and received and the incidence of bad and doubtful debts.

5   **Provide information** – tell relevant people in the practice about significant outstanding accounts and potential bad debts, and recommend the action which should be taken.

6   **Recover the monies owing** – use debt recovery methods that are appropriate to individual case and in line with the practice's procedures to recover monies owing.

7   **Be firm** – deal with debtors firmly and courteously and only write off bad or doubtful debts after weighing all the factors and consulting relevant people within the practice.

8   **Use external agencies** – do not hesitate to use, where appropriate, outside specialists such as debt collection or factoring agencies to implement the practice's credit control policies effectively.

7

Managing resources

Managing resources is about obtaining and using physical resources – supplies, equipment, services, and premises – in the most efficient way.

It involves:

(*Note:* For advice on obtaining services in the context of 'Case management' see also page 103 in Chapter 4 ('Managing client relationships').

7.1 Managing physical resources

This section is about making sure that the practice uses physical resources, such as equipment, supplies, services, energy and premises, efficiently in order to achieve the practice's key objectives.

The checklists will help you to:

- identify and secure the resources you need for the practice;
- monitor the use of resources;
- make the most effective use of physical resources.

The process for 'Managing physical resources' looks like this:

Securing physical resources	**148**

▼

Using physical resources effectively	**149**

■ Securing physical resources

1 **Get people involved** – encourage members of the practice and your team to identify what resources are needed.

2 **Use your experience** – when drawing up resource plans, take account of the way that resources have been used in the past.

3 **Consider trends and developments** – look at what is happening at the moment and factors that are likely to affect resource usage in the future.

4 **Develop consistent resource plans** – check that your plans are in line with your practice's key objectives and with legal requirements.

5 **State the resources that are needed** – base your estimates on past experience, current trends and developments and factors likely to affect resource usage in the future.

6 **Show the benefits** – state clearly the potential benefits arising from the use of the planned resources.

7 **State your assumptions** – make it clear what assumptions you have made and why.

8 **Present your plans enthusiastically** – demonstrate the commitment and drive of those who will be using the resources.

9 **Negotiate where necessary** – be prepared to adapt your plans, but ensure that you have sufficient resources to support all the activities within your control.

10 **Amend your plans** – where you cannot secure all the resources that you need, amend your plans appropriately and agree these changes with all concerned.

■ Using physical resources effectively

1   **Share responsibility** – encourage the members of the practice and your team to take individual and collective responsibility for using resources efficiently.

2   **Monitor quality** – check your product or service resources continuously to ensure that they are of a consistent quality.

3   **Monitor use** – check the use of resources against plan and make sure that your monitoring methods are reliable and comply with your practice's requirements.

4   **Take corrective action** – where the actual or potential use of resources is significantly different from your plan, take appropriate action; this may mean altering activities, modifying the way that the practice or your team use resources or renegotiating your resource allocation.

5   **Use resources efficiently** – this will, among other things, minimise any potential negative impact on the environment.

6   **Improve your use of resources** – continuously look for ways of using resources more efficiently and implement any changes promptly.

7   **Keep accurate resource records** – recording usage will help you to identify problems and plan the use of resources better in the future.

7.2   Selecting suppliers

This section is about selecting suppliers for any commodity, product or service. Note that specific advice on obtaining services in the context of 'Case management' is contained on page 103 in Chapter 4 ('Managing client relationships').

The checklists will help you to:

- draw up a list of potential suppliers;
- obtain bids or tenders that can be evaluated accurately and fairly;
- clarify any points in offers that are unclear;
- select the most appropriate offer;
- improve offers where possible.

The process of 'Selecting suppliers' looks like this:

Choosing and appointing suppliers	151

▼

Clarifying and improving offers	152

■ Choosing and appointing suppliers

1   **Develop selection criteria** – develop these in line with the practice's key objectives and specific needs.

2   **Identify potential suppliers** – draw up a list of potential suppliers so that the number and range of suppliers invited to quote provides the basis for a sufficient selection and choice.

3   **Draw up a clear specification** – check that it conforms exactly with your requirements and set out the specification and conditions of contract clearly and accurately.

4   **Invite selected potential suppliers to bid or to tender against the specification** – ask for bids or tenders in a standard format.

5   **Set the timetable** – provide clear and full information about the timetable and procedures for submitting bids or tenders and check that they are respected.

6   **Obtain sufficient bids or tenders** – make sure that adequate competition has been secured to provide a basis for a good choice of supplier.

7   **Resolve queries** – deal with queries from potential suppliers promptly and fairly.

8   **Evaluate offers and document your decision** – evaluate the bids or tenders received against established criteria and fully document your decision and the reasons for it.

9   **Communicate the decision** – communicate your decision to users, suppliers and other interested parties.

10 **Make use of performance rating** – if the practice is using a system of rating the performance of suppliers, use this accurately and fairly.

■ Clarifying and improving offers

1 **Resolve variances** – resolve any queries over variances from specification promptly.

2 **Obtain advice** – ask users and, if appropriate, technical staff, about the implications of any variances.

3 **Raise queries** – raise any queries about variances from the specification promptly with the supplier and record them accurately.

4 **Determine the scope and content of any negotiation** – consult the bid or tender specifications and the terms and conditions of contract to discover your rights.

5 **Negotiate improvements** – negotiate improvements to conditions of supply which may include price, quantity, quality standards, carriage and delivery, maintenance and after-sales service, method of payment and terms of payment; record these improvements in writing and confirm them to the supplier.

8

Managing information

This section is about ensuring that information is made available through information technology systems in order to run the practice efficiently. It is about the use of that and other information. As the management of information is the key to successful meetings, it is about leading and participating in meetings.

Managing information involves:

8.1 Introducing information technology

The Law Society's Practice Management Standards provide that practices should have an information technology strategy. This section is about selecting and monitoring information technology systems to provide the right information to manage the practice.

The checklists will help you to:

- identify the information needed;
- identify how information should flow within the practice and with the outside world;
- choose the best systems for the needs of the practice;
- implement these systems effectively within the practice;
- check that the systems are working properly and deal with any problems.

The process of 'Introducing information technology' looks like this:

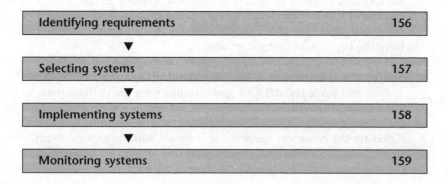

Identifying requirements	156
Selecting systems	157
Implementing systems	158
Monitoring systems	159

■ Identifying requirements

1   **Consider the fields in which information technology is relevant to the practice** – understand the range of options and applications open to the computerised law office to handle such matters as accounting, financial control, time-recording and billing, word processing, the client database, case and knowledge management, and the external and internal communications systems.

2   **Consult** – ask those who will be using the systems or who are affected by them about their requirements.

3   **Research the requirements** – consider:

   ■ the range of information and level of detail required;
   ■ the purpose of the system, who needs access, how and how quickly;
   ■ confidentiality and restrictions on access.

4   **Carry out a cost/benefit analysis** – only consider introducing a new system, or an upgrade of an existing system, if the benefits will bring a measurable return on the investment.

5   **Be cautious** – when considering any new system, ensure that it is capable of meeting the requirements of the practice both now and in the future, and note that existing systems are often under-utilised or have the capacity of being upgraded.

6   **Specify the requirements** – set out exactly what is required from the system and agree the detailed specification with the defined users of the proposed system.

7   **Calculate the resources needed** – and obtain authority to use them.

■ Selecting systems

1 **Settle the selection criteria** – draw up clear criteria and agree these with the users and others involved or affected by the proposed system.

2 **Appreciate the benefits of the different types of system** – there is a normally a very wide range of options available and you may need technical advice to guide you.

3 **Evaluate viable systems** – only consider systems that are capable of meeting your specified requirements and that are within your budget.

4 **Weigh up the benefits and disadvantages** – carefully assess the pros and cons of all the viable systems.

5 **Select** – choose the best system for your purpose and that which most closely meets your defined specification.

6 **Develop an implementation plan** – settle a detailed plan for implementing the new system and agree it with the users and others involved with or affected by the new system.

■ Implementing systems

1   **Prepare an implementation plan** – and share your carefully prepared plan with users and others involved or affected by the system.

2   **Get people involved** – encourage users and others involved to make effective and creative contributions to the implementation process.

3   **Maintain morale** – improve the efficiency of your practice by over-coming any anxieties and fears of personnel and maintain job satis-faction during the implementation of any new system; do this by seeing that users and others understand the system and their role in its implementation; gain the support of users and others by selling the benefits of the new system both for the practice and for its members.

4   **Understand the full implications of the system** – study the needs for effective procedures, quality systems and security measures and see that consideration is given to health and safety measures, as there is legislation concerning repetitive strain injuries, VDU screens and ergonomics.

5   **Train the users** – do not overlook the importance of structured train-ing and development when introducing a new system.

6   **Provide back-up and parallel systems** – systems do not always work as expected first time, so consider retaining any manual and other sys-tems currently in use until you are satisfied with the new installation.

7   **Ensure sufficient resources** – make sure that you have sufficient resources to allow the implementation to take place within the agreed time-scales.

8   **Monitor the implementation** – check that the milestones and staged targets in your plans are being met and, if there are problems, take action to resolve them so that you implement the new system on time, within budget and to the specifications agreed.

■ Monitoring systems

1   **Get users involved** – encourage users and others involved or affected by the system to provide feedback on the effectiveness and performance of the system.

2   **Monitor regularly** – establish and follow regular and formal monitoring procedures to evaluate the system concerned against agreed measures and criteria.

3   **Take account of trends and developments** – look for trends in performance in order to anticipate problems and seek to keep yourself informed of developments in technology which may help you to solve problems or enhance the system.

4   **Deal with problems** – modify the system appropriately to overcome any problems that have been identified.

5   **Gain support for improvements** – present the results of monitoring and evaluations and make your recommendations for improvements to system design or usage in a way that attracts the support of users and others involved in or affected by the system.

8.2 Using information

This section is about obtaining, using and presenting information to aid decision-making.

The checklists will help you to:

- identify and obtain the information needed;
- record and store the information in a way which makes it easy to retrieve;
- use information to forecast future trends and developments;
- analyse and evaluate the value of information;
- present information and provide advice to others;
- take decisions that are complex or critical to the practice.

The process of 'Using information' looks like this:

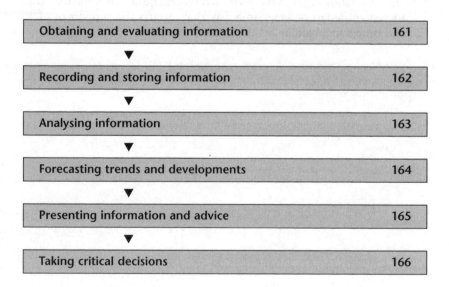

Obtaining and evaluating information	**161**
▼	
Recording and storing information	**162**
▼	
Analysing information	**163**
▼	
Forecasting trends and developments	**164**
▼	
Presenting information and advice	**165**
▼	
Taking critical decisions	**166**

■ Obtaining and evaluating information

1 **Respect internal sources of information** – the Law Society's Practice Management Standards provide that practices will have documented arrangements (informal or otherwise) which foster communication within the practice, and encourage suggestions for improvement; use this information.

2 **Identify what information is required** – give consideration regularly to the kind of information the practice is going to need (and this will be more extensive than that relating to law or money!).

3 **Review your sources of information** – review a wide range of sources of information, and consider how useful, reliable and cost-effective they are.

4 **Develop your networks** – establish, maintain and develop contacts with people who may be able to provide useful information.

5 **Seek out all relevant information** – make sure you have information on all relevant factors affecting current or potential operations.

6 **Try alternative ways of getting information** – if you are having trouble getting information from one source, try a different route.

7 **Get clear information** – if the information is ambiguous or contradictory, challenge it until the information is clear and accurate.

8 **Collect information in time for it to be of use** – make sure information arrives before the deadline.

9 **Present information in a suitable form to aid decision-making** – use summaries, diagrams and recommendations to help in decision-making.

10 **Draw appropriate conclusions** – make sure conclusions are fully supported by the relevant information and reasoned argument.

11 **Review methods of obtaining information** – review methods on a regular basis and improve them where necessary.

■ Recording and storing information

1   **Record information accurately** – check the quality of records.

2   **Record information in appropriate detail** – the practice will need to keep different amounts of detail, depending on how significant the information is and how it anticipates using it.

3   **Record and store information using accepted formats, systems and procedures** – the practice may have developed formal procedures and systems for storing different types of information, both paper-based and on computer.

4   **Make sure information can be retrieved promptly when required** – consider how urgently the information may be needed.

5   **Review methods for recording and storing information** – re-evaluate methods, systems and procedures on a regular basis, at least annually, to check that they are as effective and efficient as possible and that information technology systems are used when appropriate.

6   **Introduce new methods of recording and storing information as needed** – on a regular basis, review whether the supply of information continues to meet requirements.

7   **Analyse and correct any breakdowns in the methods of recording and storing information** – when systems break down, analyse the cause, and take action to ensure similar breakdowns do not recur.

8   **Comply with legal requirements** – ensure that the practice's systems for recording, storing and providing information meet legal and professional requirements for confidentiality.

■ Analysing information

1   **Be clear about the objectives** – question the objectives of the analysis and decide upon the decisions to be made.

2   **Select appropriate information** – get accurate information that is relevant to the objectives of the analysis and sufficient to arrive at a reliable decision.

3   **Choose appropriate methods** – use methods that are suitable to achieve the objectives of the analysis.

4   **Identify patterns and trends** – from the information try to discern any patterns and trends that are indicated.

5   **Draw conclusions** – from the analysis draw any relevant conclusions and make sure that these are supported by reasoned argument and appropriate evidence.

6   **Differentiate between fact and opinion** – when presenting the results of the analysis, make it clear what is fact and what is opinion or interpretation.

7   **Keep complete records** – provide an audit trail of the assumptions and decisions made at each stage of the analysis.

■ Forecasting trends and developments

1   **Base forecasts on the best information available** – make sure you are using the best information given the constraints of time and cost.

2   **Make forecasts of trends and developments at an appropriate time** – you will need to make some forecasts prior to planning; other developments may require forecasts to be regularly updated.

3   **Provide suitable quantitative information for decision-making** – include in forecasts sufficient quantitative information to allow you, and your colleagues to make decisions about allocating resources.

4   **State the assumptions underlying forecasts** – clearly state assumptions and the reasons for them.

5   **State the degree to which you are certain of forecasts** – highlight those areas which are most risky, or where there is little evidence to support your forecast.

6   **Illustrate the impact of trends and developments** – show how these trends will affect operations and the achievement of the practice's objectives.

7   **Review your forecasts** – analyse the reasons for any inaccuracies in forecasts, and use this information to improve future forecasts.

■ Presenting information and advice

1   **Communicate** – seize opportunities to disseminate information and advice.

2   **Make sure your information is current, relevant and accurate** – prepare carefully what you are going to say and check it with colleagues or specialists.

3   **Maintain confidentiality** – make sure that you do not divulge information that is confidential.

4   **Check that advice is consistent** – check with colleagues or specialists to ensure that your advice is accurate and complies with the procedures of the practice.

5   **Support your advice** – where appropriate, provide reasoned argument and evidence to support advice.

6   **Think about the audience** – put yourself in the audience's position, think what information it needs and present it in a manner, and at a level and pace which is appropriate.

7   **Check that the audience has understood** – ask questions and use feedback to check that the audience has understood the information presented.

8   **Improve your presentations** – use feedback from the audience to improve the way that you present information and advice.

■ Taking critical decisions

1   **Involve others** – think who could usefully contribute to the decision-making process and consult them in time for their views and advice to be taken into account.

2   **Base the decision on reliable information** – make sure that you have sufficient qualitative and quantitative information on which to base the decision and that your analysis of this information is valid.

3   **Assess the risks** – where there is incomplete or contradictory information, assess the likelihood of events not turning out as anticipated, in order to understand and to minimise the risks involved.

4   **Take consistent decisions** – see that the decisions are consistent with previous decisions and with the practice's mission statement, key objectives and current procedures.

5   **Take decisions in good time** – make sure that the decision is taken in time for appropriate action to be taken.

6   **Communicate** – think about those who need to know of the decision and make sure that you communicate the decision so that they are informed clearly and promptly.

7   **Review the decision** – periodically review the results of your decision and the process by which it was taken in order to improve decision-making in the future.

8.3 Meetings

This section is about leading and participating in meetings.

The checklists will help you to:

- be clear about the purpose of the meeting and make sure its objectives are achieved;
- prepare and make your contributions effectively;
- encourage contributions from all participants;
- take decisions.

This section covers:

Leading meetings	**168**

▼

Participating in meetings	**169**

■ Leading meetings

1   **Be clear about the purpose of the meeting** – do not call a meeting if there is a better way to exchange information, consult or inform people, solve a problem or make a decision.

2   **Invite the appropriate people to attend** – only invite those people who have something to contribute or gain, but make sure you invite all the people needed.

3   **Allow time for preparation** – prepare the manner in which you will lead the meeting with care, and talk to other members; circulate papers in advance, so everyone can be well prepared.

4   **State the purpose of the meeting at its outset** – check that all those attending understand the reasons for which they are present.

5   **Allocate sufficient time** – set a fixed time for the meeting to begin and end and allocate time appropriately for each item under discussion.

6   **Encourage all present to contribute** – use questions and individual encouragement to ensure that all views are represented.

7   **Discourage unhelpful comments and digressions** – be firm, but sensitive, in asking those present to keep to the purpose of the meeting.

8   **Summarise** – summarise the discussion at appropriate times and allocate action points at the end of each item.

9   **Take decisions** – make sure that decisions are within the meeting's authority, that they are accurately recorded, and promptly communicated to those who need to know.

10 **Evaluate the meeting** – allow time at the end of the meeting to evaluate whether the purpose of the meeting has been effectively achieved.

■ Participating in meetings

1   **Prepare carefully** – get any relevant papers and information in advance; consult others whom you are representing so that your contribution to the meeting is well prepared.

2   **Contribute effectively** – present your contributions clearly, accurately and at the appropriate time.

3   **Help to solve problems** – think about how you can help to identify problems and suggest solutions which will help the meeting to arrive at a valid decision.

4   **Keep to the point** – remember what the purpose of the meeting is and do not digress.

5   **Acknowledge the contributions and viewpoints of others** – acknowledge the contributions of others and discuss these constructively, even if you disagree with them.

6   **Represent your group effectively** – if you are at the meeting to represent the practice or your team, do not just represent your own personal views: make sure that you present fully the views of those you represent.

7   **Follow up actions points** – at the meeting or at the end of it, make a note of the points you need to action and make sure that you do so within any agreed time scale.

8   **Communicate decisions and information** – inform those who need to know about the decisions of the meeting, but keep confidential information confidential.

Reference

National Management Standards

What are the national Management Standards?

National Occupational Standards have been developed for virtually all work roles in the UK. As explained in the Preface, these standards describe what people are expected to do and how they are expected to perform.

The Management Standards describe best practice in management in the UK today. They provide *performance criteria* so that individual managers and their organisations can assess how close they come to this benchmark. The Management Standards also specify *knowledge and understanding* – the information, principles, methods and techniques – and *personal competencies* – the skills, behaviours and attitudes – which managers need to develop and demonstrate if they are to be effective.

The concept of Management Standards is very powerful as it allows practising managers whose performance is not meeting the required standard to diagnose the cause, and identify their development needs precisely. Conversely, it allows those responsible for preparing individuals for management roles to ensure that they develop all the required knowledge and skills.

The Management Standards are divided into various key roles.

Key Role A: 'Manage activities' describes the manager's work in managing the operation to meet customers' requirements and continuously to improve its performance.

Key Role B: 'Manage resources' describes the manager's work in planning and using physical resources effectively and efficiently. Physical resources include money, premises, capital equipment, energy, supplies and materials. They do not include people or information which are dealt with under separate key roles.

Key Role C: 'Manage people' describes the work of all managers in getting the most from their teams. It covers recruiting, training, building the team, allocating and evaluating work, and dealing with people problems. It also includes managing oneself and relations with others at work.

Key Role D: 'Manage information' describes the manager's role in obtaining, analysing and using information effectively to take decisions. It also covers leading and contributing to meetings.

Key Role E: 'Manage energy' describes the role of those managers with special responsibility for ensuring the organisation develops and implements policies for using energy in the most efficient way.

Key Role F: 'Manage quality' describes the specialist role of the quality manager, covering total quality management, quality assurance and quality control.

Key Role G: 'Manage projects' describes the role of those responsible for planning, controlling and closing out projects to the client's satisfaction.

Key Role H: 'Manage environmental performance' describes the role of those managers with a specific responsibility for ensuring that their organisation develops, implements, monitors and evaluates policies which are sustainable and for minimising negative impacts on the environment.

The Management Standards, like all national occupational standards, have been developed for assessment purposes, particularly assessment leading to National Vocational Qualifications (NVQs) and Scottish Vocational Qualifications (SVQs). Managers who can demonstrate that they perform to the Management Standards can be awarded an NVQ or SVQ at the appropriate level:

Strategic managers	NVQ/SVQ Level 5 (Strategy)
Operational managers	NVQ/SVQ Level 5 (Operations)
First line managers	NVQ/SVQ Level 4
Supervisors	NVQ/SVQ Level 3
Team leaders	NVQ/SVQ Level 2

The NVQ process is illustrated below. However, many organisations and their managers are using the Management Standards for a much wider range of purposes, including recruitment and selection, training needs analysis, design of training programmes, performance review and appraisal, succession planning and promotion criteria. Organisations are now linking them to quality initiatives such as ISO 9001:2000, the European Excellence Model, Best Value and Investors in People.

The checklists in this guide are based largely on the Management Standards as well as other relevant national occupational standards, such as those in accounting, customer service, marketing, purchasing and training and development. In their adaptation for the legal profession, due regard has been given to the Lexcel Practice Management Standards.

For further information about the Management Standards and how to use them, contact the Management Standards Unit, details on page xii.

The NVQ process

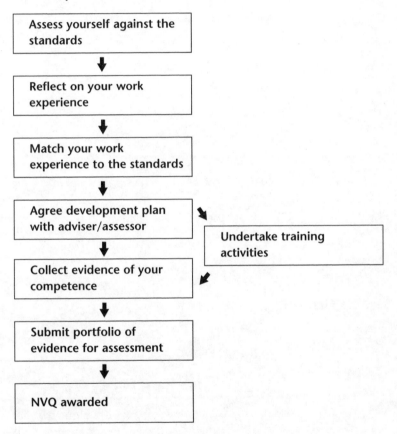

Practice Management Standards

A Management structure

A1   Practices will have a written description of their management structure which designates the responsibilities of individuals and lines of accountability. There will be a named supervisor for each area of work (a supervisor may be responsible for more than one area). The supervisor must have appropriate experience of the work supervised and be able to guide and assist others.

A1.1 The management structure should be appropriate for the partners, principals and staff, the size of the practice, its location, and the type of work it does.

A1.2 Practices should be able to explain their management structure, for example to incoming partners, principals or staff, and the written description may for example:

(a) list the designated responsibilities of individuals in the practice (including responsibility for adherence to these Standards);
(b) name committees (if any) and summarise their terms of reference;
(c) describe reporting structures in the practice, for example by including a 'family tree'.

A1.3 Supervisors should be able to describe their experience and the ways in which they guide and assist those under their supervision.

B Services and forward planning

B1   Practices will document:

(a) key objectives for 12 months and an outline strategy covering a further two years to provide a background against
which the practice may review its performance and may take
decisions about its future (plans must identify the resources
and skills necessary to deliver the strategy, with a finance
plan and budget; plans must include an information
technology strategy);

(b) the services they wish to offer and how services are to be
provided; the client groups to be served, how services are to
be provided and the way in which services are designed to
meet client needs;

(c) their approach to marketing;

(d) reviews of all elements specified in B1 at least every six
months.

Practices may choose the format and level of detail of documentation that suits them best.

B1.1 This documentation need not be disclosed to third parties.

Strategy

B1.2 The strategy should be sufficient to provide a framework for decisions about, for example, capital expenditure (including computers),
office location, staffing, strategic and business risks facing the
practice, changes in the external environment and targeting new
business, but need not be written in considerable detail.

B1.3 Most practices will already have agreed annual budgets, financial targets, etc. (as well as views about how the practice ought to develop)
and these provide a useful starting point for strategy planning. A
finance plan may consist of a projected profit and loss account in
detail for one year and in outline for the subsequent two years.

B1.4 Practices may wish to consider the following:

(a) setting goals for the practice for the coming five years;

(b) adopting a 'practice purpose statement' describing the long-term
aims of the practice.

Services

B1.5 How the practice provides services will depend upon its clients and services. Issues may include location of offices, physical access to the premises, languages spoken, facilities for clients, electronic communication, etc. These issues should normally be addressed in the practice's strategy.

Marketing

B1.6 A marketing plan should form part of the practice's strategy. For those satisfied with their current quality and level of business, a marketing plan will need to be less detailed than for a practice wishing to expand, develop a new specialism, or uncertain about its future client base. For some areas of work, the plan may need to describe how to contain demand to an acceptable level (rather than how to encourage additional business), taking account of that work's profitability and the resources of the practice.

B1.7 A marketing plan may:

(a) describe the services to be provided and client groups to be served, how services will be delivered, and the practice's client care policy;
(b) describe the practice's resources including skills and knowledge;
(c) set out objectives for the clients or business to be developed, which should be measurable and related to a time frame;
(d) explain how the structure or personnel or organisation of the practice will need to develop if those objectives are to be attained;
(e) provide a timetable for marketing activities and a budget;
(f) allocate and describe appropriate individual responsibility for the marketing activities;
(g) describe arrangements for monitoring response to the marketing effort (for example recording sources of referrals, etc.).

Non-discrimination

B2 **Practices will document procedures on non-discrimination, and have regard to guidance on non-discrimination in accepting instructions from clients and the provision of services issued by the Law Society from time to time.**

See also D8.

C Financial management

Responsibility

C1 Practices will document responsibility for financial affairs.

Financial information

C2 Practices will be able to provide documentary evidence of the following:

 (a) annual budget (including, where appropriate, any capital expenditure proposed);
 (b) quarterly variance analysis of income and expenditure against budget;
 (c) annual profit and loss account;
 (d) annual balance sheet;
 (e) annual cash flow forecast;
 (f) quarterly variance analysis of cash flow.

C2.1 In addition, practices may find it helpful to maintain the following management information (but note that it will not be practicable to produce much of this in the absence of full computerisation):

 (a) separate capital expenditure budget;
 (b) weekly or monthly aged list of debtors;
 (c) analysis of the cost of services (including apportioned overheads);
 (d) analysis of cases by category;
 (e) analysis of cases by client name;
 (f) analysis of fees by fee-earner;
 (g) analysis of fees by category or department;
 (h) analysis of working capital.

C2.2 Note that practices will not normally disclose financial information to third parties; but, for example, they may in appropriate cases instead make available an accountant's certificate that systems to provide the relevant information within the practice itself are in place.

Computerisation

C2.3 Implementation of a computerised accounting system will assist cost-effectiveness. It is unlikely that most practices could comply with these Standards in the absence of computerisation. Practices will note that B1(a) requires an information technology strategy.

C2.4 Computerised accounting systems can maintain financial records as required by the Solicitors Accounts Rules and provide other reports and information as well. Details are given in the Law Society's directory publication: *Software Solutions*.

C2.5 There is a significant cost in money and time attached to planning for development of information technology, including purchase of software, training and support following implementation. But, if properly planned, this investment will be worthwhile.

Time-recording

C3 Practices will have a documented system that ensures that time spent on casework can be properly recorded and attributed.

C3.1 The system may provide that some matters or types of matter need not be subject to time-recording (for example, where a fixed fee has been agreed) and in that case time-recording should be carried out on a sample basis.

D Managing people

Job descriptions

D1 Practices will document the skills, knowledge and experience required of fee-earners and other staff, the tasks they are required to perform, usually in the form of a written job description; but employment contracts may reserve job flexibility.

D1.1 Practices may prepare a personnel plan to help ensure that skills, knowledge and experience within the practice are developed to meet needs indicated in the forward planning documents (see B).

Recruitment

D2 Practices will have documented arrangements which evaluate the skills, knowledge and experience possessed by applicants for posts in the practice, and their integrity and suitability.

D2.1 For example, applicants may be sent a copy of the job description and a form to complete; and the contents of completed applications may then be checked against the requirements in the job description; and questions at interviews may be related to the completed application and to the job description.

New post-holders

D3 Practices will have documented arrangements to provide an induction process for new post-holders.

Objectives and performance appraisal

D4 Practices will have documented procedures to:

(a) record the responsibilities and objectives of each partner, principal and member of staff in the practice;
(b) evaluate performance of staff at least annually against those responsibilities and objectives;
(c) record in writing the performance appraisal, the record to be kept confidential to the practice and to the post-holder.

Training

D5 Practices will have documented arrangements to ensure that:

(a) all partners, principals and staff are trained to a level of competence appropriate to their work;
(b) training and development needs are assessed for each person against the objectives of the practice and are reviewed at least annually;
(c) skills and knowledge required for the management and organisation of the practice (as well as for legal practice) are provided for in training and development;
(d) appropriate written training records are maintained.

D5.1 Practices should also ensure that for cost-effectiveness and to maximise development of the practice's own resources, skills and knowledge acquired by fee-earners and other staff are communicated within the practice through training in-house.

Communications

D6 Practices will have documented arrangements (informal or otherwise) which foster communication within the practice, and encourage suggestions for improvement.

Supervision

D7 Practices will ensure that there are appropriate documented arrangements for supervision (supervision of casework is the subject of F10).

Equal opportunity

D8 Practices will document procedures on equality of opportunity including recruitment and employment procedures and have regard to guidance on equality of opportunity issued by the Law Society from time to time.

See also B2.

E   Office administration

Responsibilities

E1 Practices will document the facilities needed to provide services including:

(a) maintenance and support services;
(b) health and safety conditions;
(c) annual review of risk.

E1.2 Issues addressed in the review of risk in relation to facilities should include health and safety considerations.

Forms and procedures

E2   Practices will maintain an Office Manual collating information on office practice, which must be available to all members of the practice. There will be documented procedures to:

    (a) note each page with the date and/or number of issue;
    (b) review the Manual at least annually;
    (c) update the Manual and record the dates of amendments.

E2.1 Precedents for office forms and procedures are offered in the Law Society's *Lexcel Office Procedures Manual*.

Legal reference material

E3   Practices will have documented arrangements to ensure that:

    (a) fee-earners have ready access to up-to-date legal reference material for the areas in which the practice offers a service;
    (b) fee-earners receive timely information about changes in the law, practice and procedure relevant to their work.

F   Case management

Systems

F1   Practices will have documented arrangements to:

    (a) maintain an index of matters;
    (b) facilitate identifying any conflict of interest;
    (c) monitor the number and type of matters undertaken by each fee-earner to ensure that they are within his or her capacity;
    (d) maintain a back-up record of key dates in matters;
    (e) ensure proper authorisation and monitoring of undertakings given on behalf of the practice;
    (f) ensure proper risk management procedures are in place, including:
        (i)   appointing an overall risk manager for the practice;
        (ii)   maintaining information about the generic risks associated with the type(s) of work carried out;
        (iii) listing and defining types of case which are likely to fall within acceptable risk levels;

(iv) listing and defining types of case which are likely to fall outside acceptable risk levels;

(v) implementing procedures to manage all cases which fall outside acceptable risk levels, including mitigating actions and contingency plans, where appropriate;

(vi) conducting an annual documented review of all risk assessment data generated within the practice.

F2 Where required to do so by a third party funding the legal costs of a matter, or by a client instructing the practice in a number of matters, the practice will have a system which enables all relevant matters to be identified.

Client care

F3 Practices will have written procedures to ensure compliance with the Solicitors Costs Information and Client Care Code 1999 and to provide for clear and regular communication with clients, third parties and the court as necessary in relation to costs.

They must:

(a) inform clients of the basis of charging;

(b) provide the client with advance costs information including:

(i) the best information possible about the likely cost, including a breakdown between fees, VAT and disbursements;

(ii) where time spent is a factor in the calculation of the fees, a clear explanation of the time likely to be spent in dealing with the matter;

(iii) agreeing a fixed fee; or giving a realistic estimate; or giving a forecast within a possible range of costs;

(iv) informing the client if any estimate or quotation is not intended to be fixed, and if charging rates may be increased;

(v) explaining to a private paying client that the client may set an upper limit on the firm's costs, which may be reached without further authority;

(vi) explaining to the client the reasonably foreseeable payments which may be required to be paid to the solicitor or to a third party, and when those payments may be needed;

(vii) arrangements for updating costs information and informing the client at regular intervals (at least every six months);

(viii) whether the client may be eligible for any public funding, and if so, the costs implications for the client, particularly in relation to the statutory charge, where applicable;

(ix) whether the client's liability for costs may be covered by insurance or another party, e.g. a trade union;

(x) whether the client's liability for another party's costs may be covered by insurance.

F3.1 Practices may use standardised checklists to ensure appropriate information is obtained and given at each stage of a matter.

At the outset of a case

F4 Practices will establish a documented procedure for taking instructions which will ensure that fee-earners:

(a) agree and record:
   (i) the client's instructions and objectives;
   (ii) a clear explanation of issues raised and the advice given;
   (iii) action to be taken by the practice and likely timescale;
   (iv) strategy decided upon and any case plan;
   (v) the name and status of the person dealing with the matter and the name of the person responsible for its overall supervision and whom to contact about any problem with the service provided;

(b) confirm these with the client (ordinarily in writing);

(c) provide written information to the client about complaints procedures;

(d) identify key dates in the matter and record these in the file and in the back-up system;

(e) discuss with the client whether the likely outcome will justify the expense or risk involved, including, if relevant, the risk of having to bear an opponent's costs;

(f) consider whether there is any unusual degree of risk to the practice associated with the matter and record this on the office file;

(g) implement procedures to manage risk to the practice assessed at unacceptable levels in accordance with the practice's documented procedures.

Progress of the matter

F5   Practices will have documented procedures to ensure that:

(a) information on progress of the matter (or reasons for lack of progress) is given to the client at appropriate intervals;

(b) information about changes in the action planned to be taken in the matter, strategy or case plan, its handling (including person with conduct), or cost, is given to the client promptly;

(c) the client is informed in writing of any circumstances which will or may affect the degree of risk involved or cost benefit to the client of continuing with the matter;

(d) a timely response is made to correspondence and telephone calls;

(e) information on cost, and in publicly funded cases, the effect of the statutory charge if any, is given to the client in writing at least every six months and timely reference is made to the client when an agreed limit on costs or stage in progress is approached;

(f) in litigation matters information about adverse costs orders is given to the client immediately as payment may be required forthwith;

(g) a case plan may also be prepared in a complex matter, agreed with the client and periodically reviewed and updated.

Documents, etc.

F6   Practices will have documented procedures to ensure that they are able to identify and trace all documents, correspondence and other information relating to a matter and that these are properly stored and are readily accessible.

At the end of the case

F7   Practices will have documented procedures to ensure that at the conclusion of the matter, the practice:

(a) reports to the client on the outcome and explains any further action that the client is required to take in the matter and what (if anything) the practice will do;

(b) accounts to the client for any outstanding money;

(c) returns to the client original documents and other property belonging to the client if required (save for items which are by agreement to be stored by the practice);

(d) if appropriate, advises the client about arrangements for storage and retrieval of papers and other items retained (in so far as this had not been dealt with already, for example, in terms of business);

(e) advises the client whether he/she should review the matter in future, and if so, when;

(f) carries out a concluding risk assessment in relation to the case;

(g) notifies the practice's overall risk manager if the final assessment differs from the initial assessment, and provides a written explanation.

Services from others

F8   Practices will establish a documented procedure for using barristers, expert witnesses, etc. in providing the practice's legal services which will include provision for the following:

(a) use of clear selection criteria which should not discriminate in relation to gender, sexual orientation, race, disability or religion;

(b) where appropriate, consultation with the client in relation to selection, and proper advice to the client on choice of advocate;

(c) maintenance of records (centrally, by department, or by office) on barristers and experts used;

(d) giving of instructions which clearly describe what is required (and which, in litigation matters, comply with the rules of court and any court orders);

(e) checking of opinions and reports received to ensure they adequately provide the information sought (and, in litigation matters, comply with the rules of court and any court orders);

(f) payment of fees.

File management

F9 Practices will have documented arrangements to ensure that:

(a) the status of the matter and action taken can be easily checked by other members of the practice;

(b) documents are arranged in the file in an orderly way;

(c) key information is shown clearly on the file (for example at the front of the file) which will include details of any undertakings given on behalf of the practice.

File review

F10 Practices will have documented arrangements to supervise the conduct of casework, and these will include:

(a) availability of a supervisor to guide and assist others;

(b) appropriate procedures to allocate work in relation to the qualifications and experience of fee-earners and their workloads;

(c) arrangements for the management of case files to be reviewed periodically and the review will (except where there is only one fee-earner in the practice) be carried out by a fee-earner who has not been involved in the day-to-day conduct of the matter;

(d) a record of the review to be kept on the case file and on a central record;

(e) arrangements to ensure that any corrective action identified is carried out promptly.

F10.1 It will be a matter for each practice to determine the frequency of such reviews and whether all files are reviewed or a sample selected.

F10.2 Practices may also adopt other arrangements to ensure appropriate supervision of casework. Options include:

(a) checking incoming post;

(b) outgoing post signed by supervisor;

(c) regular review sessions with a supervisor, covering:

    (i)   new cases taken on, and discussion of 'case plans' in complex cases;

    (ii)   progress review for current cases;

    (iii) evaluation of outcomes of completed cases;

    (iv) consideration of training needs in relation to legal knowledge and skills.

Complaints

F11 Practices will have documented arrangements for complaints handling, including:

(a) **definition of a complaint;**

(b) **making the complaints procedure accessible to all clients, and providing a copy of the complaints procedure on request;**

(c) **reporting and recording centrally every complaint made by a client;**

(d) **responding appropriately to any complaint within a defined timetable;**

(e) **identifying the cause of any problem of which a client has complained, offering any appropriate redress, and correcting any unsatisfactory procedures;**

(f) **an annual documented review of any complaints to establish issues where client care may be improved, including clients' perceptions of the procedure itself.**

Further reading

Multi-media

The following are available for purchase exclusively through the Law Society Business Centre (020 7320 5640). Further information can be obtained through the Law Society's Practice Excellence Unit (see page xii for details).

Practice Excellence – Client Care Training Package CDROM/Video (Law Society 2000). This includes

- Client service – the key to success
- The solicitor–client relationship

Software Solutions: A Guide to Legal Software (Law Society).
This directory was last mailed to firms during 2000.

Books on practice management from Law Society Publishing

The books listed below are available at the Law Society Business Centre and all good book shops, or by direct mail through Marston Book Services (01235 465656). For further information on these and other titles published by Law Society Publishing, please see the website at **www.publishing.lawsociety.org.uk** or phone for a catalogue (020 7316 5599).

Please note that the *Lexcel Assessment Guide* (Law Society 2001) and *Lexcel Office Procedures Manual* (Moore and Dodd 2001) are also available as a pack entitled the *Lexcel Practice Excellence Kit.*

Adler, Mark (1990) *Clarity for Lawyers.*
Adam, Lucy (due 2001) *Marketing your Law Firm: A Solicitors' Manual.*
Bawdon, Fiona; Wignall, Gordon; and Napier, Michael (eds) (due 2001) *Conditional Fees – A Survival Guide* (second edn).
Law Society (1999) *The Guide to the Professional Conduct of Solicitors* (eighth edn).
—— (2001) *Lexcel Assessment Guide* (second edn).
—— (2001) *Solicitors' Accounts Manual* (eighth edn).
Moore, Matthew and Dodd, Michael (2001) *Lexcel Office Procedures Manual* (includes disk).
Moore, Matthew (2001) *Quality Management for Law Firms.*
Otterburn, Andrew (1998) *Profitability and Financial Management: A Guide for Medium-Sized and Smaller Legal Practices.*
—— (ed.) (1998) *Cash Flow and Improved Financial Management.*
Smith, Martin (1995) *Setting Up and Managing a Small Practice.*
Stapeley, Sue (1995) *Media Relations for Lawyers.*
Terrett, Andrew (1999) *The Internet: Business Strategies for Law Firms.*

Other publications

Boutall, Trevor (1997) *The Good Manager's Guide*, The Management Standards Unit.

Index

Time management 41

Time-recording system 135

Training and development 55–62
assessments 61
coaching 57, 59
equal opportunities 57, 58, 86
evaluating and improving 62
in-house training 56
individuals 57
introducing a programme 56
mentor, acting as 57, 60
setting objectives 43
skills, developing 43
teams 58

Values
practice, of 21, 32
work, in 75

Work
allocation 69
environment 64
planning 68

Working relationships 73–9
colleagues 78
conflicts 78, 79
encouraging collaboration 74
promoting values in work 75
reporting relationships 76
team relationships 77

Solicitors' Accounts Manual

9th Edition

The Law Society

The *Solicitors' Accounts Manual* contains all the information that solicitors' staff and reporting accountants require to ensure that firms comply with the Law Society's Solicitors' Accounts Rules.

The ninth edition has been fully updated to take account of all the latest changes to the rules, including:

- the treatment of standard monthly payments and other regular payments from the Legal Services Commission
- the retention of digital images of paid cheques
- the Solicitors Disciplinary Tribunal finding against the use of client accounts to provide banking facilities, helping to reduce the risk of money laundering.

This user-friendly manual has been prepared by the Law Society of England and Wales. It will prove invaluable to all legal practice management and accounting staff.

Available from Marston Book Services:
Tel. 01235 465 656.

1 85328 907 8
132 pages
£24.95
July 2004

The Law Society

Conveyancing Handbook

12th Edition

General Editor:
Frances Silverman

The most reliable, accurate, and up-to-date source of information and guidance on all aspects of conveyancing practice, specifically designed to give busy practitioners answers to everyday questions. Specific elements new to the 12th edition include:

- a new chapter on Licensing
- the Stamp Duty Land Tax guidance and rates
- the Solicitors' Practice (Conveyancing) Amendment Rules 2005
- revisions to Part 1 of the CML Lenders' Handbook
- an outline of the Land Registry's plans for e-conveyancing
- an introduction to Home Information Packs.

Key features:

- written in a user-friendly and accessible style
- comprehensive coverage of each step of a conveyancing transaction
- includes all the guidance on conveyancing from the Law Society
- includes the complete Solicitors Practice Rules (with consolidated amendments)
- directory of essential contacts, including: land registries, probate registries and search providers.

Available from Marston Book Services:
Tel. 01235 465 656.

1 85328 928 0
1344 pages
£79.95
October 2005

The Law Society

Becoming a Partner

5th Edition

Young Solicitors' Group

This practical book provides detailed advice on the pros and cons of accepting salaried or equity partnership. Written by young solicitors who have recently become partners, the guide tells you what to ask, what to look for and what you can realistically expect when going into partnership.

It outlines the systems and procedures that a successful and forward thinking partnership should have in place and explains the relevant tax, insurance, pensions and investment issues in plain English.

Partnership can be a rewarding career choice and this guide will help the reader reach an informed decision and negotiate a partnership deed that meets his or her needs and expectations, thus ensuring a fulfilling and secure future in the profession.

Available from Marston Book Services:
Tel. 01235 465 656.

1 85328 841 1
120 pages
£19.95
January 2003

The Law Society

Solicitors
and the Accounts
Rules

A Compliance Handbook

Peter Camp

Although the Solicitors' Account Rules
1998 have been mandatory for all
practices since May 2000, it is still common for breaches of the Rules,
to result in qualifications on accountants' reports. This clear and handy
guide explains the requirements of the Rules, providing practical
guidance on how to prevent some of the most common pitfalls.

The text outlines the basic requirements of the Solicitors' Accounts
Rules, ensuring a thorough understanding of what is required of
solicitors' practices before moving on to address the systems and
procedures that can be put in place to ensure that practices are compliant.
Key points are illustrated throughout using practical examples.

Pertinent for all solicitors' practices, this is an excellent guide to have
at hand.

Available from Marston Book Services:
Tel. 01235 465 656.

1 85328 939 6
320 pages
£49.95
June 2006

The Law Society

Family Law Protocol

2nd Edition

The Law Society

This authoritative set of best practice guidelines has been fully updated, revised and extended. Produced by the Law Society with Resolution, the Legal Services Commission and the Department for Constitutional Affairs, this is the text for family law practitioners to follow.

The second edition of this indispensible book updates the Protocol with particular changes to the sections on cohabitation, domestic violence and mediation. The changes include:

- a new section on committals
- parental responsibility for unmarried fathers under the Adoption and Children Act 2002
- changes to mediation including collaborative law and other ADR methods
- domestic violence and its effect on contact and residence applications
- the effect of the new Civil Partnership Act 2004
- new and expanded appendices

Available from Marston Book Services:
Tel. 01235 465 656.

1 85328 984 1
256 pages
£24.95
January 2006

The Law Society

Risk and Quality Management in Legal Practice

Matthew Moore and John Verry

Risk management is now a key component of law firm management. Fully up-to-date, the book takes account of the Law Society's Lexcel 2004 standard, the new money laundering regime and proposed changes to the conflict of interest rules.

The book features:

- how quality management standards also offer the prospect of improved management effectiveness, increased competitiveness and better profitability
- detailed consideration of money laundering and file closure
- expert guidance on quality management principles in general, and the Law Society's Lexcel scheme in particular.

The authors possess extensive experience of law firm management in a wide range of firms, the workings of the legal indemnity insurance industry, and the role of all the main quality standards in improving law firm performance.

Available from Marston Book Services:
Tel. 01235 465 656.

1 85328 947 7
200 pages
£39.95
March 2005

The Law Society